Technically Involved

Technology-Based Youth Participation Activities for Your Library

Linda W. Braun

American Library Association
Chicago   2003

LINDA W. BRAUN is an educational technology consultant with LEO: Librarians & Educators Online. In her job she works with schools, libraries, and other types of educational institutions to help them figure out the best way to integrate technology into their programs and services. She is also an adjunct faculty member at Lesley University in the Technology and Education graduate program and at the University of Maine, Augusta, in the library and information technology distance education program. Her books include *Teens.Library: Developing Internet Services for Young Adults* (ALA, 2002) and *Hooking Teens with the Net* (Neal-Schuman, 2003). A companion website for *Technically Involved* is available at http:// www.leonline.com/techinvolved/.

The paper used in this publication meets the minimum requirements of American National Standard for Information Sciences—Permanence of Paper for Printed Library Materials, ANSI Z39.48-1992. ∞

Library of Congress Cataloging-in-Publication Data

Braun, Linda W.
    Technically involved : technology-based youth participation activities for your library / Linda W. Braun
        p. cm.
    Includes bibliographical references and index.
    ISBN 0-8389-0861-6
    1. Libraries and teenagers. 2. Technology and youth. 3. Young volunteers in community development. 4. Volunteer workers in libraries. I. Title.
    Z718.5.B69 2004
    027.62'6—dc21   2003012021

Printed in the United States of America

07 06 05 04 03   5 4 3 2 1

CONTENTS

APPENDIXES

PREFACE

At a workshop for Young Adult Library Services Association (YALSA) Serving the Underserved (SUS) trainers, Deborah Taylor, school and student services coordinator at the Enoch Pratt Free Library, said, "Youth participation is a scary thing to librarians."[1] There is no doubt that's the case, and the reason is obvious: If done in a way that supports adolescent development, youth participation asks the librarian to change the interaction between teens and librarian. The teens and the librarian work together. Everyone makes decisions, not just the librarian.

So there might be fear at the outset. And when you add technology to the process, youth participation becomes even more frightening. Not only do librarians then have to be concerned about managing a process in which teens have a large say in how things go, but they also have to manage a process that integrates something else with which they might not be comfortable—computers and the Internet.

One could say that it's asking a lot to expect librarians to incorporate youth participation activities into their programs and services and to focus on activities that use technology. But really, it's not, and chapter 1 explains why. That chapter covers what youth development is and how youth participation fits into that construct. It also looks at the reasons why librarians should consider adding technology to an activity they look at with trepidation even when technology isn't involved.

Many librarians understand why youth participation is an important thing for libraries to do, but they aren't sure how to get started. Chapter 2 takes that into account and presents some guidelines for developing youth participation programs in the library.

But this book is not a how-to manual on youth participation. While it does provide some basics on that topic, it is really a book about how and why to integrate technology into youth participation projects at the library. Chapters 3–6 offer specific ideas for technology-based library youth participation projects. Each of the four chapters is devoted to a specific type of youth participation project and provides an overview of that genre as an introduction to suggested activities. For example, chapter 5 includes information about adolescent literacy development and its connection to the use of technology in youth participation projects. Following the introduction are outlines for three activities teens might participate in. Each activity outline includes:

- a list of the ways in which teens might be involved
- information on how the activity meets teen developmental assets (see appendix A)
- ideas for training and skill development teens might need
- a checklist of roles and responsibilities

Although this book includes a number of suggested activities, it's important to remember that in youth participation—as discussed in chapters 1 and 2—teenagers need to be allowed to initiate and develop activity ideas on their own. (The librarian takes on the role of guide and facilitator.) That means the activities outlined in chapters 3–6 should be used as jumping-off points for what might happen in any one library. While the librarian might suggest one or more of the activities in these chapters, teens should have the chance to choose which activities they want to be involved in. (A full list of the activities follows the preface, and more information on the topics discussed in *Technically Involved* is available on the companion website at http://www. leonline.com/techinvolved.)

There are different levels of youth participation. While a librarian's goal might be to have full participation in which teens initiate and implement and she simply facilitates and guides, that isn't always possible, at least in the beginning. That's why each activity outline includes the Ladder of Participation and a checklist of roles and responsibilities. The librarian should use these aids to track the level of participation she is able to achieve and to plan for future efforts based on where the current activities fall on the ladder.

The activities outlined in chapters 3–6 provide opportunities for librarians to work with teens on information literacy skills. When reading through the activities, consider where it is possible to integrate evaluation skills, research skills, critical thinking skills, and so on.

The final chapter looks at some of the barriers librarians might face in implementing technology-oriented youth participation projects. It includes ideas for helping staff feel comfortable with teen involvement in the library and for working with technology staff within and outside of the library.

The preface to the first edition of *Youth Participation in School and Public Libraries* includes this statement:

> Youth participation in library decision making means going beyond the traditional pursuit of YA input to collection building and program planning. It means giving young adults real control and responsibility for carrying out projects that meet carefully identified, significant needs. It means letting young adults set the priorities and serve their own interests, rather than manipulating them into activities which the librarian sees as useful or appropriate. This is not to say that a library should give young people free rein to do something they want, but it does call for a shift in emphasis and a more open, experimental attitude on the part of the library.[2]

That statement was written twenty years ago and still stands as the key framework for what youth participation is all about. However, something new might be added, and that's technology. Teens today need to have input not just into collection building and program planning, but also into the type of technology the library makes available, how it is made available, and how it is used. Teens need to have opportunities to use technology to create and manage the projects they work on. That's what this book is all about.

NOTES

1. Deborah Taylor, presentation at the Serving the Underserved Institute, January 23, 2003, Philadelphia, Pa.
2. Ellen Lippmann and Steve Arbuss, *Youth Participation in School and Public Libraries* (Washington, D.C.: National Commission on Resources for Youth, 1983).

YOUTH PARTICIPATION ACTIVITY LIST

CHAPTER 3

The Wired Board. Teens develop a website for a library group such as a board of trustees or Friends of the library.

Library Town Meeting. Teens facilitate an electronic chat with peers about a library issue.

CHAPTER 4

Tell Me a Story—Online. By developing a story hour website for children, teens learn children's developmental stages and creative writing, along with web design.

Online Tutorial Designers. Teens create and design instructional guides to the library's technology.

Homework Pix. Teens design and implement a workshop for younger children on using images in homework assignments.

CHAPTER 5

Fan Talk. When they develop a website on their favorite musician, book, author, or actor, teens get a chance to hone their research and evaluation skills.

Blah, Blah, Blah, Blah, Blah, Blah, Book Blog. Everybody's talking about them—weblogs, otherwise known as blogs. Why not give teens a chance to create a blog about books and authors?

Teen Guides. Discussion guides are popular with librarians and publishers. Teens who create guides for movies, books, TV shows, and so on and post them on the web are developing content that teachers and librarians can use to spark the interest of other teens.

CHAPTER 6

Wires No More. When a library is considering going wireless, teens might be just the group to research the technology and figure out the best way to implement it in the library.

Online Tour Guides. Teens design and develop content for a virtual tour of the library on the web.

The Ins and Outs of E-Mail Newsletters. E-mail may seem like an old technology at this point, but it is still a great way to get the word out about the library. In this project teens are responsible for all aspects of a library's e-mail newsletter.

ACKNOWLEDGMENTS

Many people along the way agreed to talk with me about this book on the phone, in person, via e-mail, or in a chat room. Thanks especially to Brian Simmons, Gina Macaluso, Elaine Meyers, Kimberly Bolan Taney, and Diane Tucillo for all your time and energy. Your insights into youth participation and libraries were a great help in framing this book.

Thanks also to those who were willing to brainstorm the contents of *Technically Involved* on the fly. These are the people I spontaneously asked to share their impromptu thoughts on the topics of technology, youth participation, teens, and young adult librarians. I think you all know who you are.

Once again I have to thank my ALA Editions editor, Renee Vaillancourt McGrath, who was willing to talk to me over and over and over again—in person, via e-mail, and in a chat room—about the direction of *Technically Involved*.

CHAPTER 1

Youth Participation— the What and the Why

The opening paragraph of the Young Adult Library Services Association's (YALSA) vision statement notes that "young adults are actively involved in the library decision-making process."[1] YALSA firmly supports the idea that in order to provide high-quality programs and services to teens in libraries, teens need to be involved in their planning and implementation. In the library world that involvement is referred to as "youth participation." One might wonder where this concept came from and why it is a key component of YALSA's vision statement.

YOUTH DEVELOPMENT

Youth participation is an important component of youth development. The Center for Youth Development and Policy Research defines youth development as "a process that all young people go through on the way to adulthood. It is a process or journey that automatically involves all the people around a youth—family and community. . . . Thus youth development is also a process in which family and community must actively participate."[2] As part of a teenager's community, the library must be an active participant in his or her developmental journey. One way to assist in that journey is through youth participatory activities.

YOUTH PARTICIPATION AS A PART OF YOUTH DEVELOPMENT

How does participation foster youth development? The best way to answer that question is to consider the possible outcomes from a specific youth participatory activity such as planning and implementing a computer training program for seniors. By the time the program is over, the teens will:

- Have a strong sense of competence and achievement.
- Realize they are capable of working with people other than their peers.
- Develop positive relationships with people outside of their peer group.
- Know they can help others succeed at a particular task.
- See themselves as leaders.
- Gain self-confidence and discipline.
- Understand why rules and organizational structures are needed for the delivery of programs and services.
- Comprehend the importance of delivering information so that it can be understood by those who might be different from them.

That is only a partial list of outcomes that teens achieve from just one youth participatory activity in the library. (Chapter 4 includes a full outline of this type of activity.) Activities like the one in which teens work with seniors to help the teens meet all the aspects of identity displayed in figure 1-1. Thus, the library plays an important role in a teen's journey from adolescence to adulthood.

FIGURE 1-1
Outcomes of youth development from the Center
for Youth Development and Policy Research

Aspects of Identity	Areas of Ability
A Sense of Safety and Structure High Self-Worth and Self-Esteem Feeling of Mastery and Future Belonging and Membership Perception of Responsibility and Autonomy A Sense of Self-Awareness and Spirituality	Physical Health Mental Health Intellectual Health Employability Civic and Social Involvement

Source: Center for Youth Development and Policy Research. Available at http://cyd.aed.org/whatis.html.

FIGURE 1-2
Ladder of Participation

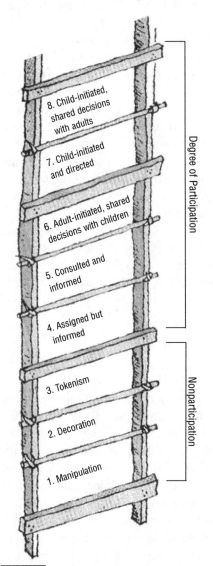

8. Child-initiated, shared decisions with adults

7. Child-initiated and directed

6. Adult-initiated, shared decisions with children

5. Consulted and informed

4. Assigned but informed

3. Tokenism

2. Decoration

1. Manipulation

Degree of Participation

Nonparticipation

Source: Roger Hart, *Children's Participation: From Tokenism to Citizenship.* Innocenti Essay no. 4 (Florence: UNICEF International Child Development Center, 1992).

YOUTH PARTICIPATION IN THE LIBRARY SETTING

The teens in the preceding example planned and implemented the computer training program for seniors. The key phrase in the previous sentence is "planned *and* implemented." Some may think that if a librarian comes up with a program idea on her own and teens attend the program it constitutes a youth participatory activity. Well, it doesn't. Some may think that if a librarian plans and implements a program based on ideas solicited from teens it constitutes a youth participatory activity. Well, it doesn't. As the Ladder of Participation in figure 1-2 illustrates, true youth participation means teens are involved in all aspects of a program, from inception to implementation.

That means teens:

- Come up with program ideas.
- Decide which ideas are best suited to library programs and services.
- Determine how to carry out their ideas.
- Work as a part of a team.
- Implement their idea in the library setting.

Youth participation in the library also means that the librarian acts not as leader, but as mentor. Teens are the leaders in the planning and implementation process. The librarian helps them as needed, advises them throughout the process, and provides support. She doesn't make the decisions; instead, she helps teens gain the skills they need to make decisions about each program or service they are developing.

Consider this example of a library youth participatory activity:

A group of teens, in consultation with a librarian, decide to teach younger children how to work with digital images so they can use these images in homework projects. In preparing for the program the teens research digital cameras, online sources for digital images, copyright laws as they relate to digital images, and software and hardware children might use when working with digital pictures. They make decisions about resources to use in the program. The teens develop the game plan for the program, create the advertising campaign and registration procedures, and lead the program they developed. They are a part of the process every step of the way. (A full outline of this type of activity appears in chapter 4.)

In this example the teens did all the work. They made all the decisions necessary to carry out the program, and then they implemented it. It's important to realize that in an activity like this, the librarian does not abdicate her responsibility to help and serve teens. By taking on the mentor role she is facilitating the decision-making process rather than making the decisions herself.

WHY TECHNOLOGY?

Helping teenagers make good decisions becomes even more important when you think about teens and technology. Teens often think they know much more about computers than adults do. In many instances they are right, but in many instances they are wrong. Teens can push the buttons on the computer without fear. They can figure out ways to get around technological glitches and failures. But they don't have the information literacy that's needed to be a truly successful user of technology.

When the librarian integrates technology into youth participatory activities she has a chance to help teens gain the skills they need to make good decisions about a wide array of technological issues. These include evaluating the quality of information, selecting resources, and distilling information for integration into a particular setting or project.

Along with helping teens gain important social, moral, emotional, physical, and cognitive competencies, outlined in figure 1-3, technology-oriented

FIGURE 1-3
Youth Development Competencies

Social Competencies, such as work and family life skills, problem-solving skills, and communication skills
Moral Competencies, such as personal values and ethics, a sense of responsibility, and citizenship (including participation in civic life and community service)
Emotional Competencies, such as a sense of personal identity, self-confidence, autonomy, and the ability to resist negative peer pressure
Physical Competencies, such as physical conditioning and endurance, and an appreciation for and strategies to achieve lifelong physical health and fitness and
Cognitive Competencies, such as knowledge, reasoning ability, creativity, and a lifelong commitment to learning and achievement.

Source: 104th Cong., S.R. 673, *Youth Development Community Block Grant Act of 1995*. Available at http://thomas.loc.gov/cgi-bin/query/F?c104:1:./temp/~c104SwyDbq:e1591.

youth participatory activities also help teens become better users of the technology that surrounds them.

When librarians implemented youth participatory activities in the past, they generally focused on books and reading. As a result, most of the teens who participated were typical library users: teens who like to read and discuss books. Teen interest in technology gives librarians a fantastic opportunity to involve people who are not typical library users. When they find out they can be members of a team creating library websites, teaching others how to use computers, repairing computers, and so on, teens who once would not have been caught dead inside of a library begin to think that it may not be such a bad place after all. One can't argue with a service that brings a whole new group of users into the library and shows them that the library is a valuable part of the community.

Remember that many technology projects enable teens to participate remotely. They might hold their planning meetings in the library or in an electronic chat room sponsored by the library. They might have to come to the library to create web pages and post them on the library's server, but maybe they can create the web pages at home and upload and download files from the same location. It is a good idea to give teens these options so those who don't feel comfortable entering the library can make their first entrance remotely and then one day walk through the doors as well.

HELPING TEENS INTO ADULTHOOD

In her introduction to the second edition of *Excellence in Library Services to Young Adults* Mary K. Chelton wrote:

> Youth participation can be viewed as a particular form of information provision, but in this form of library service the "information" is not just recorded data retrieved and transmitted through a library information system, but rather understanding and mastery of self in relation to others. This understanding is not "retrieved" for young adults by librarians; rather, youth experience it for themselves in a context provided by the library. Better understanding of themselves in relation to others is the "data" encountered in youth participation activities—a form of information that is at once personal and emotional as well as cognitive. The adolescent participant not only better understands and thinks about social bonds as a result of the library youth participation experience, but also *feels* them.[3]

What Chelton means, and what this chapter illustrates, is that by providing youth participation activities for teens librarians are helping them grow up to be successful members of society. Could there be a better answer to the question why?

NOTES

1. Young Adult Library Services Association, "Vision Statement," 1994. Available at http://www.ala.org/yalsa/about/vision.html. Accessed 25 February 2003.
2. Center for Youth Development and Policy Research, "What Is Youth Development?" Available at http://cyd.aed.org/whatis.html. Accessed 25 February 2003.
3. Mary K. Chelton, *Excellence in Library Services to Young Adults: The Nation's Top Programs,* 2d ed. (Chicago: ALA, 1997).

CHAPTER 2

Getting Teens Involved

Youth on Board, an organization that prepares young people for leadership roles in community organizations, has developed a set of guidelines to promote teen involvement in decision-making processes. This chapter looks at several of Youth on Board's points and discusses how they provide a framework for successful teen participation in technology-oriented library activities. Figure 2-1 displays those points.

FIGURE 2-1
Fourteen Points: Successfully Involving Youth in Decision Making

Know why you want to involve young people.	Recruit young people.
	Create a strong orientation process.
Assess your readiness.	Train young people for their roles.
Determine your model for youth involvement.	Conduct intergenerational training.
	Make meetings work.
Identify organizational barriers.	Develop a mentoring plan.
Overcome attitudinal barriers.	Build relationships.
Address legal issues.	Create support networks.

Source: Youth on Board, 1999.

STEPS TO SUCCESS

Assess your readiness

The first chapter of *Technically Involved* covered the why of youth participation in libraries, but even if a young adult librarian understands the reasons for starting such activities, she might not be ready to get them going. What does it take to be ready? Readiness means not only clarity on the librarian's part about the purpose of the activity; it also means making sure that library staff members and the community are open to the well-planned and active involvement of teens in library decision making. Following are some key components of readiness.

STAFF KNOWLEDGE OF TECHNOLOGY

It's OK if the staff working with teens on a technology-oriented youth participatory project are not technology experts. However, staff members do need to facilitate teen development of the activity, so they have to be open to learning new things. They can't be afraid of technology, and they must be willing to let teens take the lead in working with the technology that is going to be used in the program or service. That might mean letting go of fears around teen technology use, such as breakage, loss, damage, and so on.

BUY-IN FROM STAFF RESPONSIBLE FOR LIBRARY TECHNOLOGY

As Elaine Meyers, children's and youth manager of the Phoenix Public Library, put it, "The IT (information technology) department has to be involved in the process from the beginning."[1] Imagine that a group of teens decide they would like to help develop plans for wireless Internet access in the teen area of the building. They want to research wireless technologies and develop a proposal for what the library should purchase and how it should integrate wireless into its programs and services. (See chapter 6 for a complete outline of this type of activity.) But what if this library has a technology coordinator who is usually responsible for developing proposals of that type? Can the librarian working with the teens go ahead with the project without getting the support of the technology coordinator? She most certainly cannot, unless she wants the project to fail. That means the librarian must work with the IT staff to come up with a plan that will work for them and for the teens who are going to be working on the project. (Barriers to success related to staff buy-in is one topic covered in chapter 7.)

LIBRARY POLICIES RELATED TO USE OF TECHNOLOGY IN THE LIBRARY

What if the library has a policy that says chat is not allowed on library computers? The teens want to start a program that will enable them to talk in real time with other teens in libraries around the country about youth participation possibilities. Can the program be implemented without a change in the library policy? Doubtful. So, in order for the youth participatory activity to get under way, the library has to review and revise its policy, which is a library's legally binding document. This process is a perfect opportunity for teens to get involved in an aspect of library management and could include a presentation by the teens to the library's governing body.

GETTING BEYOND ASSUMPTIONS ABOUT TEENS AND TECHNOLOGY

"We all have stereotypes about young people," notes Youth on Board in a recent publication. "To work with young people, we must recognize these negative assumptions and learn to share real authority."[2] What stereotypes do adults have about teens when it comes to technology? Do they assume that teens will steal, break, or in some way wreak havoc on the computers? Do they assume that all teens care about is chatting, playing games, and listening to music? If the answer to these questions is yes, then it is important to disprove those assumptions by giving teens a strong technology-oriented role in the library.

Library staff might not be the only ones who hold assumptions about teens or who need to accept the importance of involving teens in technology-oriented activities. Trustees, school superintendents, principals, community IT departments, and so on may also need to be considered. Make a list of all of the people within and outside of the library who might play a role in making the proposed activity a success and set up a meeting with them to talk about what is being planned. Don't forget to involve teens in this part of the process so that the adults can see firsthand the positive role teens can play in planning and implementing library programs and services.

Determine your model for youth involvement

Figure 2-2 shows several models for technology-based youth participation in the library, but which framework is best? For example, does it make sense to start a teen technology advisory board? Should the library provide stipends

FIGURE 2-2
Models of Youth Participation

Ad hoc	Perhaps it's not possible for the library to have teens work regularly on technology-oriented projects. In that case it might work best to use an ad hoc approach. The teens won't always be working on technology projects, but when they, in consultation with the library, decide on something that is right for their skills the library staff will be ready to have them take it on. This works well as an offshoot of a library's existing teen advisory board. Perhaps some of the projects the board decides to tackle will be technology based. Wires no More, an activity in which teens select wireless technology for the library, outlined in chapter 6, would work well as an ad hoc project.
Technology-based teen advisory committee	Is it time for the library to create a formal youth group devoted to technology projects? The group might focus on a specific area of technology—say the library's website—or they might act as technology floaters in the library, working on different technology projects that benefit the library patrons or the library infrastructure. This model works best when the library can sustain ongoing technology support provided by teens along with a regular schedule of meetings, training, and so on. The Blah, Blah, Blah, Blah, Blah, Blah, Book Blog activity, in which teens develop and maintain a book blog, outlined in chapter 5 is a model of something a technology-based teen advisory board might take on.
Volunteering	Libraries with strong volunteer programs report success with this model of technology-based youth participation. The teens can be managed by young adult services staff or by a volunteer coordinator. Whatever the management structure, if you are considering going the volunteer route it's important to remember that teens who volunteer have to be managed. Schedules need to be developed and adhered to, jobs need to be defined and completed, and so on. Homework Pix, an activity outlined in chapter 4, asks teens to develop and implement a workshop for younger children. It is a project that would work well for teen technology volunteers.
Community service credit	Many schools require that teens earn a specific number of community service credits in order to graduate. Technology-based youth participation at the library could be the perfect model for community service. Teens who earn community service credit for their work in the library will receive tangible recognition that their work met a specific need. Library Town Meeting, an activity in chapter 3 in which teens moderate a chat on library issues, is a good example of technology-based youth participation that might afford community service credit.
Stipend or salary	If a library has teen pages, perhaps the technology activities those pages become involved in can be structured so that they are youth participatory. Paying teens a stipend or salary for technology-oriented jobs is a perfect opportunity to show them how much the work they do is valued. The Wired Board activity outlined in chapter 3, in which teens develop a website for a library board or Friends group, is a good example of the stipend or salary model of participation.

or salaries for the teens who are involved? Maybe teens can receive community service credits for the project. Or perhaps it can be considered one of the volunteer opportunities provided by the library. It's important to determine which model will work best for the type of activity the teens will take part in and for the capabilities of the library. But no matter which model is selected, there are two key things to remember:

- To be truly youth participatory, an activity must involve the teens in all areas of the work, from determining what needs to be done to deciding the best way to complete a given task and carrying it through to completion.

- The teens involved in a technology-based project must feel that the work they are taking on is important and has meaning. This can be accomplished through financial remuneration, credit of some type, a certificate of participation, a party, or even a simple heartfelt thank-you.

Recruit young people; build relationships

Of course, young people need to be recruited for a library youth participatory activity, but how are you going to attract them? Will it be through word of mouth? Will it be in collaboration with community agencies? Will there be posters in the library, the local schools, and around town? What is the plan? The first step is to think about the skills and qualities the teens involved in technology-oriented youth participation need to have. Remember if this is a brand-new program it will be important for teens to be involved from the ground up. You probably won't know exactly what projects they are going to work on, so it makes sense to recruit a mix of teens who encompass a variety of skills.

Once teen prerequisites are determined, take time to identify who can assist with recruitment. Make a list of all the community agencies and organizations that might be helpful and discuss a recruitment plan with them. Developing this plan with other members of the community builds a network of relationships that will not only help to get the immediate activity off the ground, but will foster stronger ties between teens and adults in the community. (Chapter 7 discusses working with outside agencies in more detail.)

Create a strong orientation process;
train young people for their roles

Sometimes as librarians start youth participatory activities they assume that teens know exactly why they are going to work on a project and the best way to get it done. But that's not always the case. For example, let's go back to the program in which teens develop a proposal for wireless access in the teen area of the library. The teens might have decided to take that project on because they want to have wireless access in the library, but that's only one reason for undertaking this type of project. In order to do a thorough job, the teens need to explore the full range of reasons for installing wireless in the library. And unless an adult explains the library's decision-making process, what proposals are meant to accomplish, how proposals are designed, and so on, teen opportunities for success will be limited. The teens might do fine researching what products the library should purchase for wireless access, but they won't necessarily be able to transfer that knowledge into a presentation or proposal that will satisfy the library's decision makers.

To ensure success, librarians must orient teens to the goals of the project as well as the goals of the library. They also need to teach them how to develop materials, policies, and programs that will work within the library's infrastructure. Different types of technology-oriented youth participation projects require different types of training. For example, if teens decide they want to help seniors in the community master the library's technology, they will probably need to receive customer service training in order to work effectively with that population.

As teens start to develop their ideas about technology-oriented projects, facilitate a discussion that allows them to brainstorm the kinds of training they might need in order to achieve success. Then help them find ways to receive that training. Also consider writing job descriptions for the different jobs those involved in the project will have to carry out. Let the teens write the job descriptions and allow opportunities for revisions once the project begins. Figure 2-3 presents a template for writing this type of job description.

Make meetings work

Nobody wants to waste time going to a meeting where nothing is accomplished. By the same token, teens won't want to participate in a program if their efforts seem to be leading nowhere from week to week, so make sure they see regular progress when they get together to work on the technology project. The librarian might need to be proactive with administration and

FIGURE 2-3
Technology-Based Youth Participation Job Description Template

Job title:
Job responsibilities:
Technology skills/qualities required to carry out the job:
Nontechnology skills/qualities required to carry out the job:
Time commitment: ☐ Once a week   ☐ Every other week   ☐ Once a month   ☐ Other (specify)
Training required:
Other:

staff in order to help the teens accomplish what they need to. Every time they meet, the teens should report on their progress and the librarian should report on hers.

Making meetings work also means scheduling the meetings at times when teens who participate in the project are available. That requires extreme flexibility on the librarian's part. It might mean holding more than one meeting on the same topic in order to get as much participation as possible. It might even mean holding meetings virtually so everyone can be involved. Ultimately, teens and librarians need to figure out what meeting schedule works best and then take responsibility for making that schedule work.

Don't forget that teens should be involved in setting the agenda for every meeting. They should decide what needs to be accomplished and who is responsible for getting things done. They should take action as needed and report on progress. If teens are given the chance to participate in this way they are more likely to be active participants in the process.

Develop a mentoring plan; create support networks

Once the technology youth participation activity is up and running, it's likely that more teens will want to become involved. This presents a great opportunity for the teens who are already part of the activity to provide training and support to the newcomers. Librarians should work with the teens to develop a plan for adding and training new members. Give the teens the chance to develop training materials and to take part in, or lead, the training that they develop.

As more and more teens become involved in technology youth participation activities sponsored by the library, they will develop an internal network of personal and technology-related support. As stated in *Youth on Board: Why and How to Involve Young People in Organizational Decision Making,* "By being networked with other youth leaders, young people see that they are not alone in their work and that other youth care about the same issues."[3]

INCENTIVES FOR YOUTH PARTICIPATION

When someone asks what it takes to get teens involved in library programs and services the most common answer is "food." Sometimes it's said jokingly, sometimes seriously. Of course food can't hurt, but if it is a major incentive for involvement, chances of success are limited. The librarian needs to consider the guidelines outlined in this chapter and come up with a clear plan of action. If she does, the teens, the library, and the community will all gain from that initial planning process.

NOTES

1. Elaine Meyers, telephone conversation, August 13, 2002.
2. *Youth on Board: Why and How to Involve Young People in Organizational Decision Making* (Somerville, Mass.: Youth on Board, 2000), 22.
3. Ibid., 24.

CHAPTER 3

On the Road to Greatness

Just as every young person is different, so are his or her interests and passions. We might have a future Michelangelo and a future Malcolm X on the same team. Each young person needs the opportunity to cultivate greatness in his or her way.[1]

As teens move through adolescence, they frequently take advantage of opportunities that can help them achieve some level of greatness. These might include helping out at a soup kitchen, working in an after-school program, or spending time on a political campaign. What is central to teenagers' interest and participation is their need to be involved in activities that will make some difference in the world around them.

WHY GREATNESS IS IMPORTANT

This need to take part in meaningful activities is an important component of the developmental assets of adolescents as outlined by the Search Institute. (See appendix A.) In particular, the external assets related to empowerment and the internal assets that focus on positive self-identity, values, and social competence speak directly to teen involvement in meaningful community activities. Consider this story:

In February 2003, two teenage boys who are in foster care traveled to Ghana for two weeks in order to install computers, which they helped rebuild, in classrooms in the African country. The boys were part of a computer repair program at Children's Village in Westchester County New York. In a radio interview, the Children's Village staff member traveling with the boys said, "All of these trips have changed our kids in dramatic ways. Our kids have had such a low sense of themselves. . . . We spend all our time at Children's Village telling them that they can take control of their lives and their futures, and this is just a very dramatic way to experience that."[2]

The two boys on that trip were taking part in an activity that not only changed the lives of the children in the classrooms in Ghana, who now have computers, but also changed their own lives. In terms of the Search Institute's forty developmental assets, the experience would demonstrate to the teens that they were valued as a part of their community, looked upon as resources in the community, and able to serve others. In terms of internal assets, the boys learned about a culture other than their own and had a real-life opportunity that increased their sense of personal power and self-esteem.

Activities that empower teens to make positive changes in their own lives and in the lives of others are a regular part of youth participatory programming at some libraries. Suggestions include:

- Asking patrons to bring in canned goods as payment for fines. Teens then package and deliver the goods to shelters or other facilities in the community.
- Hosting programs in local shelters that are organized and led by teens.
- Having teens participate in library fund-raising campaigns by running book sales, making phone calls, or writing letters.

STRATEGIES THAT CULTIVATE GREATNESS

In their article on cultivating greatness in teens, Maura Wolf and Robert Lewis Jr. list seven strategies that support greatness:

- Promote core values.
- Provide appropriate challenges.
- Expose young people to great leaders.
- Reinforce values with daily, weekly, and monthly practices.
- Develop core competencies
- Utilize diversity as a strength.
- Provide resources and support for growth.[3]

Let's explore how librarians who are developing youth participatory activities to help teens achieve greatness can incorporate these seven strategies.

Promote core values. Determine what values the program is going to instill in teens. Those values are likely to connect to the Search Institute's developmental assets by supporting boundaries and expectations, constructive use of time, and social competencies.

Provide appropriate challenges. Understand what teens already know, what they need to know, and what they will realistically be able to achieve. For example, teens might want to rewire the entire library for high-speed access. But the librarian knows that this project will be impossible for them to accomplish because of limitations in their own skills and restrictive library policies. Therefore, it's important for the librarian to work with the teens to develop an activity that is going to be challenging but possible.

Expose young people to great leaders. Realize that librarians are role models in teens' lives. By showing teens how to work successfully with others and how to carry a project through to fruition, librarians can do a lot for their understanding of what leadership is all about. Exposure to great leaders doesn't mean teens need to work with politicians and celebrities. Most likely there are great leaders closer at hand.

Reinforce values with daily, weekly, and monthly practices. Give teens a chance to talk about what they are gaining from the participatory experience provided by the library. Make sure they regularly remind themselves of the values they are learning and how those values make a difference in their everyday lives.

Develop core competencies. Make sure teens are given the opportunity to gain the skills they need to succeed in the project. Before teens can install assistive technology devices on a library's computers, for example, they might need to be trained in installation and operating procedures for such devices. Teens need to learn the skills that will help them get to greatness.

Utilize diversity as a strength. Do not shy away from an activity because it might bring a diverse group of teens together. Librarians need to look at the activity as an opportunity to help teens understand that in order to achieve greatness one has to be ready, willing, and able to work with a diverse group of people. Technically speaking, it might be possible—via chat, instant messaging, weblogs, and so on—to promote diversity by connecting those who come to the library to those who don't.

Provide resources and support for growth. Build in opportunities for teens to talk about what has and hasn't worked in the activity. Librarians need to facilitate discussions in which teens can voice their gripes and frustrations. Once they get past their frustrations, they can move on to greatness.

HOW TO DO IT:
TEMPLATES FOR YOUTH PARTICIPATION
PROGRAMS THAT SUPPORT GREATNESS

The next section of this chapter looks at two technology-based youth partic-ipatory activities that help teens achieve greatness. Each activity includes information on how it supports the developmental assets that relate to great-ness in teens, suggestions for levels of participation, and information on the training teens might need in order to achieve success. It might not be possi-ble to achieve the highest level of youth participation (as shown on the lad-der of participation) in any one activity, but working with the materials pro-vided should help place the activity in the top half of the ladder.

The Wired Board

This activity gives teens the chance to create a website for a library board of trustees or Friends of the Library group.

WHERE'S THE YOUTH PARTICIPATION?

Teens who participate in this activity might:

- Decide for whom to develop a website—the library board, the Friends of the Library, or both.
- Develop criteria for evaluating sites on the same topic.
- View similar sites to evaluate what works and what doesn't.
- Attend meetings of the group(s) chosen.
- Decide what materials to include on the website.
- Develop the materials for the site.
- Write the content.
- Design the site.
- Code the site.
- Maintain the site.
- Advertise the site.
- Evaluate the final site and the process of creating the site.

WHY WOULD TEENS WANT TO DO IT?

By getting involved in the work of the library's governing body or support organization, teens get to be a part of the behind-the-scenes activities of the library. Teens taking part in this activity would have access to people, technology, and areas of the library that are not readily accessible to their peers. They would work on web content or design that would be published for all members of the community to see. Their names would be associated with a project beneficial to an organization that needed their help.

WHAT DOES IT HAVE TO DO WITH GREATNESS?

Teens involved in this type of activity help library-related groups communicate who they are and what they do. Teens have to consider what topics are important to the community at large in order to make decisions about the materials to post on the library website. They also have to consider how the materials should be displayed in order to create a view of the organization that connects what they do, who they are, and their role in the library. By attending meetings of the selected organization, teens see firsthand how meetings are run, what skills are required to effectively run a meeting, and how decisions are made by a group.

WHAT DEVELOPMENTAL ASSETS DOES IT MEET?

See appendix A for more information on the developmental assets for adolescents.

Community values youth	Youth as resources	Service to others
Adult role models	Positive peer influence	High expectations
Creative activities	Youth programs	Responsibility
Planning and decision making	Interpersonal competence	Personal power
Self-esteem	Sense of purpose	Positive view of personal future

WHO HAS THE RESPONSIBILITY?

The following checklist outlines the various tasks that need to be accomplished in order to carry out this activity. Use it to determine the level of participation teens will have, who will be responsible for the various steps in the process, and where each task needs to be accomplished. Some tasks might require checking more than one box.

Task	Who Is Responsible?	Where?
Decide to take on the project	☐ Teens ☐ Librarian ☐ Other Notes/Comments	☐ On site ☐ Remote Location
Determine website topic—what group will be the focus?	☐ Teens ☐ Librarian ☐ Other Notes/Comments	☐ On site ☐ Remote Location

Task	Who Is Responsible?	Where?
Develop site evaluation criteria	☐ Teens ☐ Librarian ☐ Other *Notes/Comments*	☐ On site ☐ Remote Location
View similar sites for ideas	☐ Teens ☐ Librarian ☐ Other *Notes/Comments*	☐ On site ☐ Remote Location
Develop project timeline	☐ Teens ☐ Librarian ☐ Other *Notes/Comments*	☐ On site ☐ Remote Location
Assign project roles	☐ Teens ☐ Librarian ☐ Other *Notes/Comments*	☐ On site ☐ Remote Location
Attend meetings	☐ Teens ☐ Librarian ☐ Other *Notes/Comments*	☐ On site ☐ Remote Location
Develop site materials	☐ Teens ☐ Librarian ☐ Other *Notes/Comments*	☐ On site ☐ Remote Location

Task	Who Is Responsible?	Where?
Write site content	☐ Teens ☐ Librarian ☐ Other *Notes/Comments*	☐ On site ☐ Remote Location
Code the site	☐ Teens ☐ Librarian ☐ Other *Notes/Comments*	☐ On site ☐ Remote Location
Maintain the site	☐ Teens ☐ Librarian ☐ Other *Notes/Comments*	☐ On site ☐ Remote Location
Advertise the site	☐ Teens ☐ Librarian ☐ Other *Notes/Comments*	☐ On site ☐ Remote Location
Evaluate site content and development process	☐ Teens ☐ Librarian ☐ Other *Notes/Comments*	☐ On site ☐ Remote Location
Other	☐ Teens ☐ Librarian ☐ Other *Notes/Comments*	☐ On site ☐ Remote Location

After looking through the checklist, where would you put this youth participatory activity on the Ladder of Participation that is shown in figure 3-1?

IS TRAINING NECESSARY?

The teens' level of participation in this activity will determine the type of training and skill development needed. The following table outlines a few of the areas in which teens might need support.

Activity	Training/Skill Development Required
Attend meetings	Meeting management, note-taking, and decision-making skills
Present information to a group of adults	Public speaking skills, technology presentation skills (for example, PowerPoint), negotiating skills
Design a group website	Knowledge of web design principles
Develop a website	Knowledge of HTML or website development software, understanding of file and folder structure, ability to upload and download files

THE BOTTOM LINE

A project like The Wired Board benefits teens, the library, the library's board of trustees or Friends group, and the entire community. Teens learn something about the inner workings of the library and its decision-making process. Adults who work in the library or are members of the board or Friends group discover that teens can be successful members of their community. Community residents get a chance to use technology to find out what the library is working on. At the same time, they see that the library respects teenagers and is willing to help them develop skills that will lead to success in their adult lives. The Wired Board integrates technology with a meaningful participatory activity that helps teens gain leadership skills that will come in handy on the road to greatness. This is true whether the teens become involved in the project after the librarian makes initial contact with the adults or whether they work on every aspect from the ground up.

FIGURE 3-1
Ladder of Participation

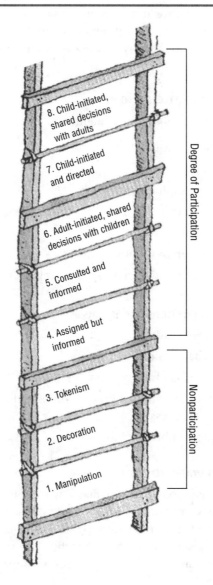

8. Child-initiated, shared decisions with adults

7. Child-initiated and directed

6. Adult-initiated, shared decisions with children

5. Consulted and informed

4. Assigned but informed

3. Tokenism

2. Decoration

1. Manipulation

Degree of Participation

Nonparticipation

Source: Roger Hart, *Children's Participation: From Tokenism to Citizenship.* Innocenti Essay no. 4 (Florence: UNICEF International Child Development Center, 1992).

Library Town Meeting

In this activity teens organize and facilitate a chat session for peers to discuss a specific library policy, service, or program. Following the chat session they make recommendations to the library administration based on the content of the discussion.

WHERE'S THE YOUTH PARTICIPATION?

Teens who participate in this activity might:

- Select the topics to discuss.
- Research chat software.
- Develop software evaluation criteria.
- Evaluate chat software.
- Select chat software.
- Raise money to purchase software.
- Research the library and teen perspective related to the issue up for discussion.
- Come up with questions and discussion points to use in the chat.
- Facilitate the chat session.
- Advertise the chat session.
- Evaluate the success of the session.
- Write a report to present to library administration that highlights the findings of the chat session.
- Present findings to library administration.

WHY WOULD TEENS WANT TO DO IT?

Teens gravitate to electronic chat; for many, it is their preferred method of communication. They are familiar with different chat formats and software and are able to negotiate the attendant technology. Teens who take part in the Library Town Meeting activity get to use a technology they prefer while making their voices heard around a topic of interest or impact.

WHAT DOES IT HAVE TO DO WITH GREATNESS?

In this activity teens learn about decision making from the ground up. At the highest level of participation, teens would facilitate the chat session and present findings and recommendations to the library administration. In this case, it would be important for them to understand the core values and mission of the library as well as the core values of their peers who will take part in the chat. They will have to negotiate differences of opinion and build consensus so the library can make a final decision about the project, policy, or activity.

WHAT DEVELOPMENTAL ASSETS DOES IT MEET?

See appendix A for more information on the developmental assets for adolescents.

Other adult relationships	Community values youth	Youth as resources
Service to others	Adult role models	Positive peer influence
High expectations	Creative activities	Youth programs
Responsibility	Restraint	Planning and decision making
Interpersonal competence	Peaceful conflict resolution	Personal power
Self-esteem	Sense of purpose	Positive view of personal future

WHO HAS THE RESPONSIBILITY?

The following checklist outlines the various tasks that need to be accomplished in order to carry out this activity. Use it to determine the level of participation teens will have, who will be responsible for the various steps in the process, and where each task needs to be accomplished. Some tasks might require checking more than one box.

Task	Who Is Responsible?	Where?
Decide to take on the project	☐ Teens ☐ Librarian ☐ Other *Notes/Comments*	☐ On site ☐ Remote Location

Task	Who Is Responsible?	Where?
Select chat topic(s)	☐ Teens ☐ Librarian ☐ Other *Notes/Comments*	☐ On site ☐ Remote Location
Research chat software	☐ Teens ☐ Librarian ☐ Other *Notes/Comments*	☐ On site ☐ Remote Location
Develop software evaluation criteria	☐ Teens ☐ Librarian ☐ Other *Notes/Comments*	☐ On site ☐ Remote Location
Evaluate software	☐ Teens ☐ Librarian ☐ Other *Notes/Comments*	☐ On site ☐ Remote Location
Select software	☐ Teens ☐ Librarian ☐ Other *Notes/Comments*	☐ On site ☐ Remote Location
Raise funds to purchase software	☐ Teens ☐ Librarian ☐ Other *Notes/Comments*	☐ On site ☐ Remote Location

Task	Who Is Responsible?	Where?
Research issues related to chat topic	☐ Teens ☐ Librarian ☐ Other *Notes/Comments*	☐ On site ☐ Remote Location
Develop chat content— questions for discussion	☐ Teens ☐ Librarian ☐ Other *Notes/Comments*	☐ On site ☐ Remote Location
Advertise chat session	☐ Teens ☐ Librarian ☐ Other *Notes/Comments*	☐ On site ☐ Remote Location
Facilitate chat	☐ Teens ☐ Librarian ☐ Other *Notes/Comments*	☐ On site ☐ Remote Location
Evaluate chat success	☐ Teens ☐ Librarian ☐ Other *Notes/Comments*	☐ On site ☐ Remote Location
Develop report on findings and recommenda- tions	☐ Teens ☐ Librarian ☐ Other *Notes/Comments*	☐ On site ☐ Remote Location

Task	Who Is Responsible?	Where?
Present report to library administration	☐ Teens ☐ Librarian ☐ Other *Notes/Comments*	☐ On site ☐ Remote Location
Other	☐ Teens ☐ Librarian ☐ Other *Notes/Comments*	☐ On site ☐ Remote Location

After looking through the checklist, where would you put this youth participatory activity on the Ladder of Participation that is shown in figure 3-2?

IS TRAINING NECESSARY?

The teens' level of participation in this activity will determine the type of training and skill development needed. The following table outlines some of the areas in which teens might need support.

Activity	Training/Skill Development Required
Evaluate and select software	Evaluation skills
Facilitate chat	Online facilitation skills, conflict resolution skills
Develop presentation	Knowledge of word processing or presentation software (for example, PowerPoint)
Present chat findings	Public speaking skills, technology presentation skills (PowerPoint, etc.)

FIGURE 3-2
Ladder of Participation

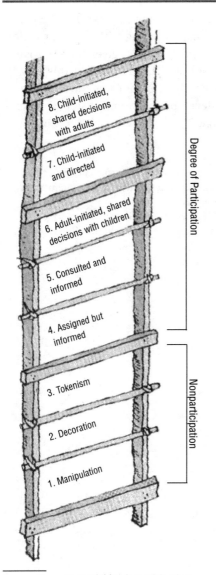

8. Child-initiated, shared decisions with adults

7. Child-initiated and directed

6. Adult-initiated, shared decisions with children

5. Consulted and informed

4. Assigned but informed

3. Tokenism

2. Decoration

1. Manipulation

Degree of Participation

Nonparticipation

Source: Roger Hart, *Children's Participation: From Tokenism to Citizenship.* Innocenti Essay no. 4 (Florence: UNICEF International Child Development Center, 1992).

THE BOTTOM LINE

Many teens love chat, and many librarians don't. However, chat is a mode of communication that can be used to great advantage to gather information and discuss issues with people who might never walk into the library building—teens, for example. By giving teens a chance to organize and participate in a chat town meeting around a topic that is important to them, librarians provide the opportunity to gain leadership skills in decision making and consensus building. If teens are a part of the decision-making process, they are more likely to buy into the decision that is ultimately made. And if their ideas play a large role in the final decision, they will certainly feel that they have played a meaningful role in the process. They will know they have contributed something to their community.

BENEFITS OF PROGRAMMING
FOR GREATNESS

Teens need to feel like they are making a difference in their world. The youth participatory activities suggested in this chapter, along with the information provided on developing leadership skills in teenagers, gives the librarian a framework to support that teen need. Wolf and Lewis stated it this way in their article on cultivating greatness in youth: "As educators, mentors, parents, and supporters of young people's development we must step up to create the conditions for greatness to emerge."[4]

NOTES

1. Maura Wolf and Robert Lewis Jr., "Cultivating Greatness," *Community Youth Development Journal* 2, no. 2 (spring 2001). Available at http://www.cydjournal.org/ 2001Spring/wolf.html. Accessed 25 February 2003.
2. National Public Radio, Morning Edition, "Foster Trip to Ghana," February 13, 2003. Available at http://discover.npr.org/rundowns/segment.jhtml?wfId=1160447. Accessed 25 February 2003.
3. Wolf and Lewis, "Cultivating Greatness."
4. Ibid.

CHAPTER 4

Bringing Generations Together

Research suggests that youth and seniors who work together strengthen their ties to the community, their sense of belonging, their interpersonal skills, and their understanding of the other generation. Youth form friendships and gain personal and professional guidance that significantly enriches their lives. They also gain a new appreciation for history, having heard some of it first-hand, and they feel good about helping older members of the community view youth with less suspicion, concern, and fear.[1]

For many years libraries have been sponsoring programs that bring adolescents together with people who are older or younger than they are. Some programs have teens read to younger children as a part of a story hour or read-a-thon event; others have them interview seniors to gather information about a particular time, place, or event in history. Sometimes seniors act as mentors to teens, helping them make decisions about life and careers. No matter how they are structured, intergenerational programs produce tangible benefits.

Looking at the Search Institute's forty developmental assets for adolescents (see appendix A), we see that library intergenerational programs can meet several of the areas outlined. Teens involved in these activities will have support from nonparental adults and a chance to serve others. Intergenerational activities create opportunities for creative activity and fill

---

HOW TO FIND INTERGENERATIONAL PROGRAM IDEAS

Generations United maintains a database of intergenerational programs. You can search the database by keyword or select from a list of program categories, including "computer skills." You can also submit your intergenerational program for inclusion in the database. Check it out at http://63.251.88.156/programs.

---

the need to act responsibly. By working with an age group other than their own in a youth participatory activity teens will gain competence both socially and in terms of planning and decision making. This in turn increases their self-esteem and gives them a sense of purpose.

WHAT DOES IT TAKE?

To create a successful intergenerational program, whether or not it includes the use of technology, it's important to plan carefully and make sure teens and those they are working with at another end of the generational spectrum are at ease in their roles. For example, if teens are teaching children or seniors how to use computers, the students must feel comfortable with a teen in the teaching role. The teens might need to learn how to train members of another age group, and the trainees might need to be educated about the positive role teens can play in the library.

On its website, the National Academy for Teaching and Learning about Aging offers the following tips for success in developing intergenerational programs:

- Clearly define educational objectives.
- Present a balanced view of older adults.
- Consider the needs of students and older adults.
- Review effective communications skills with students.
- Choose the setting carefully.[2]

Let's examine how these programming considerations fit into the library context.

Clearly define educational objectives. Know what you and the teens want to get out of the project. Is it being developed simply to give teens a chance to get to know people who are older or younger than themselves? Is the project going to help teens understand other generations so that they can be more successful in making decisions about their own lives? Is it just something a librarian thought would be fun for the teens and the seniors or younger children? Of course, not all objectives are equally valid, but the first step in determining whether the proposed project has a valid purpose is to articulate and evaluate its objectives.

Present a balanced view of older adults. Make sure teens don't have just one idea of what the group they are going to be working with is all about. For example, if they think all senior citizens are technologically challenged, that's not a balanced view. If they want to have positive, productive interactions, they need to consider all the different types of young or elderly people they might encounter.

Consider the needs of students and older adults. Think about the lifestyle of the seniors or children with whom the teens are going to be working. If teens are going to host an author chat for elementary school children, it will be important to consider when children of that age group would be available to take part in the activity. The same is true if they are going to lead training sessions for seniors on how to send e-mail. In other words, teens planning the intergenerational activity need to learn about the group they are going to work with in order to make good choices about the how, what, and when of the planned activity.

Review effective communications skills with students. This is one of the keys to successful intergenerational programming. Libraries that have teens teach seniors how to use a computer often spend time training the teens on customer service issues and effective communication strategies. Teens need to know that the way they talk to their friends isn't necessarily the way they would talk with the seniors they are training. Make sure they have an opportunity to practice their communications skills before leaping into their first intergenerational activity.

Choose the setting carefully. Maybe it's easiest to hold the intergenerational activity in the library, but that

---

TEENS, SENIORS, AND COMPUTERS

I've had great success having teens lead computer training sessions for the senior citizens of our community. We spend an hour training the teens on what types of questions and problems to expect from their pupils and how to handle these issues. Then the teens execute what they've learned in people skills combined with what they already know about computer use. Mainly, they teach the senior citizens how to use the Internet and e-mail. The main thing I focus on with the teens is to keep it simple. After the training session, the teens realize how much they know in comparison to a beginner or intermediate user.

Each teen is paired up with one senior citizen, and each twosome gets a computer. We limit our programs to ten because that's all we have room for, but we actually had a waiting list last year to do this program again, and the really great thing was that the list was ten people deep for both generations.

As the teens are teaching the seniors, I walk around and observe, but when a teen doesn't know the answer to a question, he or she calls me over and all three of us interact. I offer the teens community service volunteer hours for their participation. Our high school students need twenty hours of community volunteer service for graduation.

Source: E-mail message from Brian Simons, young adult librarian, Manitowoc (Wisconsin) Public Library, Aug. 12, 2002.

might not be the best location for the student group. For example, if teens plan on teaching seniors how to use computers they might find that holding the training in a local senior center that has a computer lab is more practical than holding it in the library. The seniors might be more comfortable in the senior center, and it might have facilities available to them that the library does not. If teens are going to work with elementary school children on creating web pages, the best place to host the sessions might be a local school with a computer lab. If the library's computers are in public access areas, or if its Internet connections are slow, help the teens find another venue that will be more conducive to teaching and learning.

HOW TO DO IT: TEMPLATES FOR INTERGENERATIONAL YOUTH PARTICIPATION PROGRAMS

Many libraries are already providing technology-based youth participatory intergenerational programs in their communities. A typical format matches seniors with teens who act as mentors and trainers as seniors learn the ins and outs of computer use. However, there are many other possibilities to use technology in these types of programs. The three activity outlines that follow illustrate what different program formats might accomplish. Each outline includes an overview of the activity, a look at the developmental assets it meets, and information on how to implement the activity at varying levels of youth participation. It might not be possible to reach the highest level of participation (as shown on the ladder of participation) in an activity, but the materials provided should help you move toward the upper levels.

Tell Me a Story—Online

This youth participatory activity encourages teens to create online story hour materials that can be used by children and their parents at home, in the library, or at school.

WHERE'S THE YOUTH PARTICIPATION?

Teens who participate in this activity might:

- Research what makes good storytelling on the web.
- Determine the age of the site's target audience.
- Research the interests of children in the site's target audience.
- Research stages of child development.
- Investigate and evaluate audio and video technologies for use on the site.
- Develop evaluation criteria.
- Evaluate other online story sites for children.
- Write stories for the site.
- Create images for the site.
- Develop the design of the site.
- Code the site.
- Post materials developed.
- Advertise the availability of the online story hour site.
- Evaluate the process and the success of the materials developed.

WHY WOULD TEENS WANT TO DO IT?

One draw for teens is the opportunity to create web content that people all over the world will access. Another is that they will be able to use different pieces of software to create the contents of the site. Another less tangible attraction is that they will be able, to some extent, to relive their own youth. Teens sometimes are seen hanging out with the toys and games in the library's children's department. They tend to make it all seem like a joke—that's how they get away with it with their friends—but many teens feel a sense of security in going back to what's familiar, whether it be toys, stuffed animals, or stories.

WHAT ARE THE POSITIVE INTERGENERATIONAL CONNECTIONS?

Aside from creating something for a group of younger children, this youth participatory activity also challenges teens to consider the best way to present stories to children using the interactive medium of the web. They will write text and design an interface that tells children and parents what's available on the site and does so in an entertaining fashion. Teens will have to learn about stages in childhood development in order to select materials for the website that are appropriate for the targeted age group.

WHAT DEVELOPMENTAL ASSETS DOES IT MEET?

See appendix A for more information on the developmental assets for adolescents.

Youth as resources	Service to others	Positive peer influence
High expectations	Creative activities	Youth programs
Caring	Responsibility	Planning and decision making
Interpersonal competence	Self-esteem	Sense of purpose

WHO HAS THE RESPONSIBILITY?

The following checklist outlines the various tasks that need to be accomplished in order to carry out this activity. Use it to determine the level of participation teens will have, who will be responsible for the various steps in the process, and where each task needs to be accomplished. Some tasks might require checking more than one box.

Task	Who Is Responsible?	Where?
Decide to take on the project	☐ Teens ☐ Librarian ☐ Other Notes/Comments	☐ On site ☐ Remote Location
Develop activity timeline	☐ Teens ☐ Librarian ☐ Other Notes/Comments	☐ On site ☐ Remote Location

Task	Who Is Responsible?	Where?
Assign roles/ responsibilities	☐ Teens ☐ Librarian ☐ Other *Notes/Comments*	☐ On site ☐ Remote Location
Research online storytelling sites	☐ Teens ☐ Librarian ☐ Other *Notes/Comments*	☐ On site ☐ Remote Location
Research children's interests	☐ Teens ☐ Librarian ☐ Other *Notes/Comments*	☐ On site ☐ Remote Location
Learn about child development ages and stages	☐ Teens ☐ Librarian ☐ Other *Notes/Comments*	☐ On site ☐ Remote Location
Develop criteria for evaluating various technologies and website components	☐ Teens ☐ Librarian ☐ Other *Notes/Comments*	☐ On site ☐ Remote Location
Investigate audio/video technologies for the site	☐ Teens ☐ Librarian ☐ Other *Notes/Comments*	☐ On site ☐ Remote Location

Task	Who Is Responsible?	Where?
Evaluate audio/ video technologies	☐ Teens ☐ Librarian ☐ Other *Notes/Comments*	☐ On site ☐ Remote Location
Evaluate online story sites for children	☐ Teens ☐ Librarian ☐ Other *Notes/Comments*	☐ On site ☐ Remote Location
Write stories	☐ Teens ☐ Librarian ☐ Other *Notes/Comments*	☐ On site ☐ Remote Location
Develop site design	☐ Teens ☐ Librarian ☐ Other *Notes/Comments*	☐ On site ☐ Remote Location
Code the site	☐ Teens ☐ Librarian ☐ Other *Notes/Comments*	☐ On site ☐ Remote Location
Create/edit site images	☐ Teens ☐ Librarian ☐ Other *Notes/Comments*	☐ On site ☐ Remote Location

Task	Who Is Responsible?	Where?
Upload site contents	☐ Teens ☐ Librarian ☐ Other *Notes/Comments*	☐ On site ☐ Remote Location
Advertise the site	☐ Teens ☐ Librarian ☐ Other *Notes/Comments*	☐ On site ☐ Remote Location
Evaluate the process and product	☐ Teens ☐ Librarian ☐ Other *Notes/Comments*	☐ On site ☐ Remote Location
Other	☐ Teens ☐ Librarian ☐ Other *Notes/Comments*	☐ On site ☐ Remote Location

After looking through the checklist, where would you put this youth participatory activity on the Ladder of Participation that is shown in figure 4-1?

FIGURE 4-1
Ladder of Participation

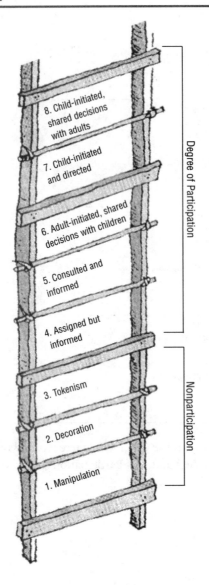

8. Child-initiated, shared decisions with adults

7. Child-initiated and directed

6. Adult-initiated, shared decisions with children

5. Consulted and informed

4. Assigned but informed

3. Tokenism

2. Decoration

1. Manipulation

Degree of Participation

Nonparticipation

Source: Roger Hart, *Children's Participation: From Tokenism to Citizenship.* Innocenti Essay no. 4 (Florence: UNICEF International Child Development Center, 1992).

IS TRAINING NECESSARY?

The teens' level of participation in this activity will determine the type of training and skill development needed. The following table outlines some of the areas in which teens might need support.

Activity	Training/Skill Development Required
Determine age level for the site and matching materials with that level	Knowledge of child development ages and stages
Develop content	Creative writing skills and knowledge of writing for the web
Illustrate content	Ability to create and edit images for the web
Design online story-hour website	Knowledge of web design principles
Develop the website	Knowledge of HTML or website development software, understanding of file and folder structure, ability to upload and download files

THE BOTTOM LINE

Teens were once children, and this youth participatory activity gives them a chance to learn something about their own childhood while at the same time improving the childhood of others in their community. Teen literacy skills will improve as they read and write stories that might be included on the website. Once started, this activity could be carried out by teens over many years. Those who started the site might then teach their peers how to maintain and update it. One day, children who read or listened to stories that the library's teens created for an online story hour might add content of their own.

Online Tutorial Designers

This youth participatory activity gives teens the chance to create online tutorials to teach children or senior citizens how to use computers.

WHERE'S THE YOUTH PARTICIPATION?

Teens who participate in this activity might:

- Decide target audience.
- Research the computer skill needs of a specific population.
- Decide the topics to cover in the online tutorials.
- Create content for the online tutorials.
- Develop criteria for evaluating online instruction
- Research methods for delivering online instruction.
- Evaluate methods of online instruction to determine which is best for their project.
- Learn software tools such as Flash to use in creating tutorials.
- Design the online tutorials.
- Code tutorials.
- Post the tutorials on the web.
- Advertise the availability of the tutorials.
- Evaluate the process and the success of the materials developed.

WHY WOULD TEENS WANT TO DO IT?

Teens don't mind hearing that they know more about technology than their parents, teachers, or local librarians. Sometimes it's even true. In this activity teens get a chance to show others what they know while at the same time learning new skills.

WHAT ARE THE POSITIVE INTERGENERATIONAL CONNECTIONS?

As teens develop the online tutorials, they will need to consider the needs of the audience for whom the materials are being created. For example, they will have to consider the special technology needs of senior citizens and the learning abilities of young children. They will also need to figure out the best way to communicate the information to a particular age group. For example, if writing tutorials for children teens might decide to include emoticons and other technology slang. That approach might not be suited to tutorials for older adults.

WHAT DEVELOPMENTAL ASSETS DOES IT MEET?

See appendix A for more information on the developmental assets for adolescents.

Community values youth	Youth as resources	Service to others
High expectations	Creative activities	Youth programs
Caring	Responsibility	Planning and decision making
Interpersonal competence	Self-esteem	Sense of purpose

WHO HAS THE RESPONSIBILITY?

The following checklist outlines the various tasks that need to be accomplished in order to carry out this activity. Use it to determine the level of participation teens will have, who will be responsible for the various steps in the process, and where each task needs to be accomplished. Some tasks might require checking more than one box.

Task	Who Is Responsible?	Where?
Decide to take on the project	☐ Teens ☐ Librarian ☐ Other Notes/Comments	☐ On site ☐ Remote Location
Develop activity timeline	☐ Teens ☐ Librarian ☐ Other Notes/Comments	☐ On site ☐ Remote Location
Assign roles/ responsibilities	☐ Teens ☐ Librarian ☐ Other Notes/Comments	☐ On site ☐ Remote Location

Task	Who Is Responsible?	Where?
Determine tutorial audience	☐ Teens ☐ Librarian ☐ Other *Notes/Comments*	☐ On site ☐ Remote Location
Research skill needs	☐ Teens ☐ Librarian ☐ Other *Notes/Comments*	☐ On site ☐ Remote Location
Determine tutorial topics	☐ Teens ☐ Librarian ☐ Other *Notes/Comments*	☐ On site ☐ Remote Location
Develop criteria for evaluation	☐ Teens ☐ Librarian ☐ Other *Notes/Comments*	☐ On site ☐ Remote Location
Research delivery methods	☐ Teens ☐ Librarian ☐ Other *Notes/Comments*	☐ On site ☐ Remote Location
Design tutorials	☐ Teens ☐ Librarian ☐ Other *Notes/Comments*	☐ On site ☐ Remote Location

Task	Who Is Responsible?	Where?
Learn software tools	☐ Teens ☐ Librarian ☐ Other *Notes/Comments*	☐ On site ☐ Remote Location
Create content	☐ Teens ☐ Librarian ☐ Other *Notes/Comments*	☐ On site ☐ Remote Location
Code tutorials	☐ Teens ☐ Librarian ☐ Other *Notes/Comments*	☐ On site ☐ Remote Location
Post on the web	☐ Teens ☐ Librarian ☐ Other *Notes/Comments*	☐ On site ☐ Remote Location
Advertise tutorials	☐ Teens ☐ Librarian ☐ Other *Notes/Comments*	☐ On site ☐ Remote Location
Evaluate process and product	☐ Teens ☐ Librarian ☐ Other *Notes/Comments*	☐ On site ☐ Remote Location

Task	Who Is Responsible?	Where?
Other	☐ Teens ☐ Librarian ☐ Other *Notes/Comments*	☐ On site ☐ Remote Location

After looking through the checklist, where would you put this youth participatory activity on the Ladder of Participation that is shown in figure 4-2?

IS TRAINING NECESSARY?

While it might not seem that writing a step-by-step guide to a specific technical skill would require training, there are aspects to the online tutorial activity that will be best achieved if teens have the chance to develop specific skills. The following table looks at a few of the skills teens might need to succeed in this project.

Activity	Training/Skill Development Required
Develop interactive content	If teens decide that the best way to present the information to the target audience is through interactivity they may need to learn Flash or another software program with similar capabilities.
Develop tutorial text	Understanding of differences between communication of formats and what is the best way to present information online
Develop tutorial images	Knowledge of web graphics and graphics software (e.g., Photoshop, Image Ready, or Photoshop Elements)
Design tutorial website or pages	Knowledge of web design principles
Create tutorial website or pages	Knowledge of HTML or website development software, understanding of file and folder structure, ability to upload and download files

FIGURE 4-2
Ladder of Participation

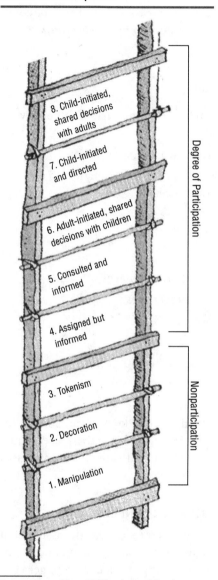

8. Child-initiated, shared decisions with adults

7. Child-initiated and directed

6. Adult-initiated, shared decisions with children

5. Consulted and informed

4. Assigned but informed

Degree of Participation

3. Tokenism

2. Decoration

1. Manipulation

Nonparticipation

THE BOTTOM LINE

Demonstrating skills, teaching others those skills, and gaining new skills all at the same time are perfect ways for teens to achieve a sense of purpose and self-esteem. They might realize that they still have something to learn about technology and that some adults know as much about it as they do. They might also discover ways to communicate effectively with community members different from them.

Source: Roger Hart, *Children's Participation: From Tokenism to Citizenship.* Innocenti Essay no. 4 (Florence: UNICEF International Child Development Center, 1992).

Homework Pix

Teens who participate in this activity develop a program to teach children how to find, edit, and create images to integrate into homework projects.

WHERE'S THE YOUTH PARTICIPATION?

Teens who participate in this activity might:

- Research copyright issues as they relate to using images in homework projects.
- Develop materials for use in the Homework Pix workshop.
- Research software that might be used to teach children how to edit and create images for use in homework projects.
- Develop software selection criteria.
- Select software for the workshop.
- Raise funds to purchase software.
- Learn how to use software to edit and create images.
- Develop and implement registration procedures.
- Lead the Homework Pix workshop.
- Advertise the workshops.
- Evaluate the workshop product, process, and success.

WHY WOULD TEENS WANT TO DO IT?

Teens like to create digital images, and many teens like to locate images for their own purposes or for homework assignments. This activity uses something teens enjoy and allows them to teach practical skills to an interested audience.

WHAT ARE THE POSITIVE INTERGENERATIONAL CONNECTIONS?

In order to succeed in this activity teens will need to analyze the assignment needs of younger children. They need to discover what's going on in elementary classrooms and what types of materials are appropriate for younger children to use in homework projects. They might even communicate with elementary school teachers to gain perspective on children's homework needs, thus bringing another generation into the mix.

WHAT DEVELOPMENTAL ASSETS DOES IT MEET?

See appendix A for more information on the developmental assets for adolescents.

Community values youth	Youth as resources	Service to others
Adult role models	High expectations	Creative activities
Youth programs	Achievement motivation	School engagement
Caring	Responsibility	Planning and decision making
Personal power	Self-esteem	Sense of purpose

WHO HAS THE RESPONSIBILITY?

The following checklist outlines the various tasks that need to be accomplished in order to carry out this activity. Use it to determine the level of participation teens will have, who will be responsible for the various steps in the process, and where each task needs to be accomplished. Some tasks might require checking more than one box.

Task	Who Is Responsible?	Where?
Decide to take on the project	☐ Teens ☐ Librarian ☐ Other *Notes/Comments*	☐ On site ☐ Remote Location
Create project timeline	☐ Teens ☐ Librarian ☐ Other *Notes/Comments*	☐ On site ☐ Remote Location
Assign roles and responsibilities	☐ Teens ☐ Librarian ☐ Other *Notes/Comments*	☐ On site ☐ Remote Location

Task	*Who Is Responsible?*	*Where?*
Research copyright	☐ Teens ☐ Librarian ☐ Other *Notes/Comments*	☐ On site ☐ Remote Location
Develop software selection criteria	☐ Teens ☐ Librarian ☐ Other *Notes/Comments*	☐ On site ☐ Remote Location
Research software for workshop	☐ Teens ☐ Librarian ☐ Other *Notes/Comments*	☐ On site ☐ Remote Location
Evaluate software	☐ Teens ☐ Librarian ☐ Other *Notes/Comments*	☐ On site ☐ Remote Location
Select software	☐ Teens ☐ Librarian ☐ Other *Notes/Comments*	☐ On site ☐ Remote Location
Raise money to purchase software	☐ Teens ☐ Librarian ☐ Other *Notes/Comments*	☐ On site ☐ Remote Location

Task	Who Is Responsible?	Where?
Develop training materials	☐ Teens ☐ Librarian ☐ Other *Notes/Comments*	☐ On site ☐ Remote Location
Develop registration procedures	☐ Teens ☐ Librarian ☐ Other *Notes/Comments*	☐ On site ☐ Remote Location
Advertise workshop	☐ Teens ☐ Librarian ☐ Other *Notes/Comments*	☐ On site ☐ Remote Location
Lead workshop	☐ Teens ☐ Librarian ☐ Other *Notes/Comments*	☐ On site ☐ Remote Location
Evaluate workshop, product, process, success	☐ Teens ☐ Librarian ☐ Other *Notes/Comments*	☐ On site ☐ Remote Location
Other	☐ Teens ☐ Librarian ☐ Other *Notes/Comments*	☐ On site ☐ Remote Location

After looking through the checklist, where would you put this youth participatory activity on the Ladder of Participation that is shown in figure 4-3?

IS TRAINING NECESSARY?

For this activity to be successful teens need to have technology skills and skills related to teaching children. The table below looks at a few of these skills.

Activity	Training/Skill Development Required
Locate images on the web	Image searching skills using search engines and other library search tools
Teach image creation and editing	Knowledge of image editing/creation software (Teens who know how to use the software might actually present a workshop on the software to other participants in this activity.)
Evaluate software	Evaluation skills
Teach children	Customer-service skills and knowledge of child development stages

THE BOTTOM LINE

Teens understand that they and younger children are required to do homework. They also understand that digital images are a good way to enhance homework projects. Put this together with the fact that teens are often very adept at locating, importing, and creating digital images, and that they like to show what they know to others, and you have a recipe for a successful youth participatory program at your library.

BENEFITS OF INTERGENERATIONAL PROGRAMMING

Technology-based intergenerational youth participatory activities in the library allow teens to show off the skills they already have, to learn new skills, and to articulate their ideas to members of a different age group. The activities discussed in this chapter are a way to get started working with teens and other generations in the community to create activities that maximize skills and support the needs of all involved.

FIGURE 4-3
Ladder of Participation

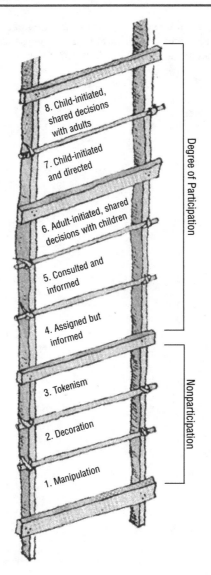

8. Child-initiated, shared decisions with adults

7. Child-initiated and directed

6. Adult-initiated, shared decisions with children

5. Consulted and informed

4. Assigned but informed

Degree of Participation

3. Tokenism

2. Decoration

1. Manipulation

Nonparticipation

Source: Roger Hart, *Children's Participation: From Tokenism to Citizenship.* Innocenti Essay no. 4 (Florence: UNICEF International Child Development Center, 1992).

NOTES

1. "Two Generations of Partners in Prevention," *Youth in Action Bulletin* 5 (July 1999): 2–9.
2. National Academy for Teaching and Learning about Aging, "Planning Intergenerational Programs." Available at http://www.cps.unt.edu/natla/web/planning_intergenerational_progr.htm. Accessed 25 February 2003.

CHAPTER 5

Reading, Writing, and Youth Participation

There is lots of conversation these days around literacy. People talk about literacy not only in general terms, but also in terms of information literacy, computer literacy, media literacy, and so on. For teenagers, literacy in its various forms is key to lifelong success. The youth participation activities covered in chapters 3, 4, and 6 include components related to technology and information literacy. This chapter, while focusing on some of those literacy areas, highlights technology-oriented activities that connect primarily with a teenager's needs in the areas of reading and writing.

ADOLESCENT LITERACY DEFINED

The International Reading Association (IRA) summarizes its position on adolescent literacy this way:

> The International Reading Association emphasizes that adolescent literacy is a continuum. The ongoing literacy development of adolescents is just as important, and requires just as much attention, as that of beginning readers. The expanding literacy demands placed upon adolescent learners includes more reading and writing tasks than at any other time in human history. They will need reading to cope with the escalating flood of information and to fuel their imaginations as they help create the world of the future. The association's recommendations for focusing on the literacy needs of adolescent learners include providing them with:
>
> • access to a wide variety of reading material that appeals to their interests

- instruction that builds the skill and desire to read increasingly complex materials
- assessment that shows their strengths as well as their needs
- expert teachers who model and provide explicit instruction across the curriculum
- reading specialists who assist students having difficulty learning how to read
- teachers who understand the complexities of individual adolescent readers
- homes, communities, and a nation that supports the needs of adolescent learners[1]

The IRA's position statement has practical implications for a library that is thinking about developing technology-based youth participatory activities that enhance literacy. It notes that teens are required to do more writing than at any other time in human history. The truth of this can be seen not only in the homework teenagers are required to complete for school, but in the resources they use in their day-to-day lives. Every time a teen goes online to take part in a chat or instant messaging conversation, every time a teen sends an e-mail message to a friend, every time a teen uses Google or another Internet search engine, he or she is required to write.

The International Reading Association's statement also notes that teens need to read in order to deal with the quantity of information they encounter daily. They need to read in order to play many of the games they use online. They need to read in order to decide which technological gadget to buy. They need to read in order to evaluate which website is best for their research needs. The need to read hasn't decreased as a result of technology; it has actually increased.

Now let's connect some of the IRA's specific recommendations to library-based youth participatory activities for teens.

Access to a wide variety of reading materials that appeal to their interests. In many libraries around the country teen advisory boards (TABs) participate in collection development projects. For example, teens might visit a local music or book store in order to make selections for the library's collection. Librarians also have teens read reviews in various journals and periodicals in order to make recommendations for the collection and they have teens select website links. These types of activities are a good way to make sure teens have access to a variety of reading materials that suit their interests.

Instruction that builds the skill and desire to read increasingly complex materials. Maybe instruction isn't what librarians think their youth participatory activities are all about. And if a youth participatory activity is designed entirely by teenagers, instruction seems to be the last thing on anyone's mind. However, the truth is, even when a librarian is "sitting back" and letting teens run the show there are opportunities to help them learn something new or to understand something in a different way. The connection to instruction might be an activity in which teens interview seniors in the community as a step in writing a town history for the library and publishing it in an electronic format. In order to carry out the interviews teens have to research the town's history and develop questions to ask the seniors. They might even require and receive training in how to conduct an interview. As part of the research process, the librarian might need to teach the teens what resources to use and how to access and read historical documents or other primary sources. In other words, she will help the teens learn to read materials that might be very different from what they regularly spend time reading.

Assessment that shows their strengths as well as their needs. Assessment is another word for evaluation. It's important to assess not only the success of the librarian's work with teens, but also the work teens do as a part of a youth participatory project. For example, consider the teens who helped select materials for the library's collection. Perhaps some of the materials selected didn't circulate well. In that case, the librarian and the teens would all need to evaluate why the selections were made and how to improve the process the next time. This is a great opportunity for the librarian who is working with teens to provide feedback on what might make the youth participatory activity more successful. A segment of the activity might include creating assessment tools for the projects, which could lead to discussion on assessment of resources in general. Teenagers definitely have to read and write to accomplish that. They also have to think carefully about what constitutes success within the project in which they are participating.

Expert teachers who model and provide explicit instruction across the curriculum. Whether or not a librarian serving young adults feels comfortable calling herself "teacher," it's important to be an expert in the field of young adult services and library service in general. That expertise allows the librarian to demonstrate to teens in youth participatory settings how to accomplish tasks successfully and how the library can provide resources and support that help teens meet their intended goal. In chapter 3 this modeling was called leadership. In this chapter the role models are termed "experts."

Consider once again the teens who help a librarian with collection development. As a part of that activity the librarian can demonstrate the processes she uses in selecting materials for the collection. She can explain the fundamentals of collection development—maybe even have the teens read the library's policy—to help them understand the role good collection development plays in a library. In the IRA's position statement on adolescent literacy the section related to expert teaching concludes with this statement:

> Expert teachers help students get to the next level of strategy development by addressing meaningful topics, making visible certain strategies, then gradually releasing responsibility for the strategies to the learners. Adolescents deserve such instruction in all their classes.[2]

To see how this relates to teen participation in collection development, replace the word "teachers" with "librarians," and change "classes" to "libraries." If the librarian gives the teens the tools they need to be successful—information about the library's collection development policy, tips for successful collection development, and the purpose of library collection development—teens involved in the project will have what they need to make responsible decisions on their own about materials to add to a library's collection, whether those materials are books, audiovisual, or websites.

Teachers who understand the complexities of individual adolescent readers. Once again, change the word "teachers" to "librarians." In this context, it means that librarians need to realize that not all teenagers are the same in terms of their reading needs and interests. In terms of youth participation it might mean that when the library sponsors a shopping spree for books for teens it also sponsors one for videos, music, and perhaps even technology. Another way to look at this is to realize that teens involved in a single youth participation activity will bring a variety of skills to that activity. So a successful activity should include tasks that use the varying skills of the teens rather than force everyone to participate in the same way.

Homes, communities, and a nation that supports the needs of adolescent learners. This is the obvious place that libraries fit into the adolescent literacy framework. As an integral part of the community, the library has a role to play in supporting teens' need for literacy development. In its position paper the IRA states that libraries can support literacy by providing homework help.[3] There's no doubt that librarians working on youth participatory activities with teens can do a lot more than provide homework support.

In a publication titled *Planning for Results,* which outlines service responses to various community needs, the Public Library Association (PLA) notes, "A library that offers basic literacy service addresses the need to read and to perform other essential daily tasks.[4] Youth participatory activities that support adolescent literacy development signal a library's strong commitment to fulfilling its role in promoting basic literacy as defined by PLA.

HOW TO DO IT:
TEMPLATES FOR LITERACY-BASED
YOUTH PARTICIPATION PROGRAMS

Probably the most common youth participatory activities that libraries already sponsor are those that enhance literacy development in some way. There are collection development activities, coffeehouse activities, magazine publishing projects, and so on. Looking through the success stories in the new edition of *New Directions for Library Service to Young Adults,* published in 2002 by the Young Adult Library Services Association, one can't help but note that each activity has a literacy connection.[5]

Youth participation projects that integrate technology also provide strong support for teen literacy development. Consider the example of teen Web Surfers at the Central Rappahannock Regional Library, who have this to say about themselves:

> The Web Surfers are Ben, Michelle, Nina, Ryan, Shona, Stanley, Lorne and anyone else in grades 7–12 who is interested. The 3rd Wednesday of every month (usually) from 7:00–8:00 we meet, we eat, we talk (a lot!), we decide what to put on the web page. Not just this page, but what Cool Links should be added.[6]

The Web Surfers actually do quite a bit more than they let on in that description. If you look at the YA Clicks column in various issues of *Voice of Youth Advocates* (VOYA), you'll find that the teens and the YA librarian, Rebecca Purdy, review websites for the column and even developed website review criteria that were published in the magazine. You can read about the development of their criteria on the VOYA website.[7]

The Web Surfers obviously use reading and writing skills in their projects. They have to read what's on the web, evaluate the quality of the content, and then write what they think. In developing criteria for evaluation they had to use a wide range of literacy skills. The young adult librarian no doubt took on several of the teaching and expert roles outlined in the IRA adolescent literacy position statement.

Almost any youth participation project teens and librarians take on will have a literacy component; it is the library, after all. The following pages present ideas for other projects that integrate literacy and technology. It might not be possible to achieve the highest level of participation, as shown on the Ladder of Participation, but these materials will help advance you to the top half of the ladder.

Fan Talk

This youth participatory activity gives teens a chance to create a fan site for their favorite author, book, movie, actor, or musician.

WHERE'S THE YOUTH PARTICIPATION

Teens who participate in this activity might:

- Decide who or what the fan site should be about.
- Research what makes a good fan site.
- Develop criteria for evaluating fan sites.
- Develop the materials for the site.
- Obtain copyright permission to use images and audio on the site.
- Write site content.
- Design the site.
- Code the site.
- Publish the site.
- Maintain the site
- Evaluate the site.
- Advertise the site.

WHY WOULD TEENS WANT TO DO IT?

A fan website gives teens a chance to tell the world about something that interests them. Instead of simply talking about the topic with their friends in their own community, teens will be able to spread the word to the world at large, thereby gaining a sense of personal power and value to the community.

HOW DOES IT SUPPORT ADOLESCENT LITERACY?

By reading other fan sites teens will access a variety of materials that relate to their needs and interests and will read materials that vary in their level of complexity. By evaluating other fan sites, along with those they create, teens will be involved in assessment activities. By helping teens determine the best way to create and present information for the site, the librarian will act as expert, guide, and model. By giving teens the opportunity to develop a fan site the library will support adolescent literacy development.

WHAT DEVELOPMENTAL ASSETS DOES IT MEET?

See appendix A for more information on the developmental assets for adolescents.

Other adult relationships	Youth as resources	Service to others
Adult role models	Positive peer influence	High expectations
Creative activities	Youth programs	Reading for pleasure
Responsibility	Planning and decision making	Interpersonal competence
Self-esteem	Sense of purpose	Positive view of personal future

WHO HAS THE RESPONSIBILITY?

The following checklist outlines the various tasks that need to be accomplished in order to carry out this activity. Use it to determine the level of participation teens will have, who will be responsible for the various steps in the process, and where each tasks needs to be accomplished. Some tasks might require checking more than one box.

Task	Who Is Responsible?	Where?
Decide to take on a project	☐ Teens ☐ Librarian ☐ Other Notes/Comments	☐ On site ☐ Remote Location
Select the topic of the site	☐ Teens ☐ Librarian ☐ Other Notes/Comments	☐ On site ☐ Remote Location
Develop a timeline for the project	☐ Teens ☐ Librarian ☐ Other Notes/Comments	☐ On site ☐ Remote Location

Task	Who Is Responsible?	Where?
Assign task/ responsibilities to group members	☐ Teens ☐ Librarian ☐ Other *Notes/Comments*	☐ On site ☐ Remote Location
Research what makes a good fan site	☐ Teens ☐ Librarian ☐ Other *Notes/Comments*	☐ On site ☐ Remote Location
Develop materials for the site	☐ Teens ☐ Librarian ☐ Other *Notes/Comments*	☐ On site ☐ Remote Location
Obtain copyright permission where necessary	☐ Teens ☐ Librarian ☐ Other *Notes/Comments*	☐ On site ☐ Remote Location
Write the site content	☐ Teens ☐ Librarian ☐ Other *Notes/Comments*	☐ On site ☐ Remote Location
Design the site	☐ Teens ☐ Librarian ☐ Other *Notes/Comments*	☐ On site ☐ Remote Location

Task	Who Is Responsible?	Where?
Code the site	☐ Teens ☐ Librarian ☐ Other *Notes/Comments*	☐ On site ☐ Remote Location
Advertise the site	☐ Teens ☐ Librarian ☐ Other *Notes/Comments*	☐ On site ☐ Remote Location
Maintain the site	☐ Teens ☐ Librarian ☐ Other *Notes/Comments*	☐ On site ☐ Remote Location
Evaluate the site, including development process and use	☐ Teens ☐ Librarian ☐ Other *Notes/Comments*	☐ On site ☐ Remote Location
Other	☐ Teens ☐ Librarian ☐ Other *Notes/Comments*	☐ On site ☐ Remote Location

After looking through the checklist, where would you put this youth participatory activity on the Ladder of Participation that is shown in figure 5-1?

IS TRAINING NECESSARY?

The teens' level of participation in this activity will determine the type of training and skill development needed. The following table outlines a few of the areas in which teens might need support.

Activity	Training/Skill Development Required
Research qualities of a good fan site	Knowledge of evaluation skills
Obtain copyright materials	Understanding of concepts of intellectual property and letter/e-mail correspondence with publishers and other professionals
Design the site	Workshop on web design principles, graphic design, and image editing/creation software
Code the site	Knowledge of HTML or web creation software. Knowledge of file and folder structure and the ability to upload and download files

THE BOTTOM LINE

Some might say that helping teens create a site in honor of their favorite author, books, TV show, movie, or musician isn't the best way to use a library's time and resources. However, if this type of project is considered in the context of the literacy development needs of adolescents, its value is obvious. Teens will be reading, writing, and evaluating. They will be communicating with their peers about something of interest. They will be using library resources to learn about a topic and to inform others about that topic. Isn't that what library resources are for?

FIGURE 5-1
Ladder of Participation

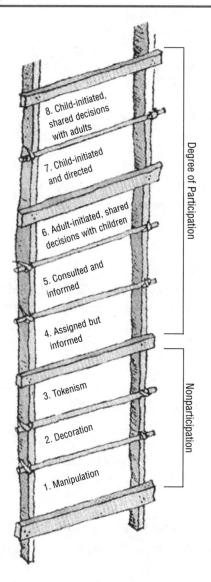

8. Child-initiated, shared decisions with adults

7. Child-initiated and directed

6. Adult-initiated, shared decisions with children

5. Consulted and informed

4. Assigned but informed

3. Tokenism

2. Decoration

1. Manipulation

Degree of Participation

Nonparticipation

Source: Roger Hart, *Children's Participation: From Tokenism to Citizenship.* Innocenti Essay no. 4 (Florence: UNICEF International Child Development Center, 1992).

Blah, Blah, Blah, Blah, Blah, Blah, Book Blog

In this activity teens create book-oriented weblogs, otherwise known as blogs. A blog is just like a journal or diary. The difference is that it is online. The person writing the blog—the blogger—regularly posts his or her thoughts and feelings about a range of topics, from relationships to school to entertainment to current events.

WHERE'S THE YOUTH PARTICIPATION?

Teens who participate in this activity might:

- Decide what books or authors to talk about on the weblog.
- Look at weblogs to determine why some work better than others.
- Develop criteria for selecting weblog software.
- Evaluate weblog software.
- Select weblog software.
- Raise money to purchase weblog software.
- Install and configure weblog software for the library's server, or set up a weblog account that doesn't require use of the library's server.
- Set up a schedule for weblog posting.
- Design the look of the weblog.
- Write the weblog entries.

WHY WOULD TEENS WANT TO DO IT?

Blogging has become a popular activity with teens, largely because they can use blogs to write about topics of interest for others to read and react to. Teens get a sense of empowerment from this activity and feel that they are making a contribution to the community by expressing their ideas and insights.

HOW DOES IT SUPPORT ADOLESCENT LITERACY?

There is no way around it: To have a blog one has to write on a regular basis. Blogs are a perfect way to get teens writing, writing, writing, and writing. They can read blogs from other teens and consider why some might be more successful than others. Was one person's writing style easier to read? Librarians who develop youth participation activities that integrate blogs can help teens at different reading and writing levels. Teens who might not feel comfortable writing in a school homework context can hone their skills in a more appealing environment.

WHAT DEVELOPMENTAL ASSETS DOES IT MEET?

See appendix A for more information on the development assets for adolescents.

Other adult relationships	Youth as resources	Service to others
Adult role models	Positive peer influence	High expectations
Creative activities	Youth programs	Achievement motivation
Reading for pleasure	Responsibility	Planning and decision making
Personal power	Self-esteem	Sense of purpose

WHO HAS THE RESPONSIBILITY?

The following checklist outlines the various tasks that need to be accomplished in order to carry out this activity. Use it to determine the level of participation teens will have, who will be responsible for the various steps in the process, and where each task needs to be accomplished. Some tasks might require checking more than one box.

Task	Who Is Responsible?	Where?
Decide to take on the project	☐ Teens ☐ Librarian ☐ Other *Notes/Comments*	☐ On site ☐ Remote Location
Develop project timeline	☐ Teens ☐ Librarian ☐ Other *Notes/Comments*	☐ On site ☐ Remote Location

Task	Who Is Responsible?	Where?
Assign roles and responsibilities	☐ Teens ☐ Librarian ☐ Other *Notes/Comments*	☐ On site ☐ Remote Location
Decide the books or authors to talk about on the blog	☐ Teens ☐ Librarian ☐ Other *Notes/Comments*	☐ On site ☐ Remote Location
Develop weblog evaluation criteria	☐ Teens ☐ Librarian ☐ Other *Notes/Comments*	☐ On site ☐ Remote Location
Evaluate teen weblogs	☐ Teens ☐ Librarian ☐ Other *Notes/Comments*	☐ On site ☐ Remote Location
Develop weblog software evaluation criteria	☐ Teens ☐ Librarian ☐ Other *Notes/Comments*	☐ On site ☐ Remote Location
Evaluate weblog software	☐ Teens ☐ Librarian ☐ Other *Notes/Comments*	☐ On site ☐ Remote Location

Task	Who Is Responsible?	Where?
Select weblog software	☐ Teens ☐ Librarian ☐ Other *Notes/Comments*	☐ On site ☐ Remote Location
Raise funds to purchase weblog software	☐ Teens ☐ Librarian ☐ Other *Notes/Comments*	☐ On site ☐ Remote Location
Install and con-figure weblog software for library server	☐ Teens ☐ Librarian ☐ Other *Notes/Comments*	☐ On site ☐ Remote Location
Set up weblog account if not using library's server	☐ Teens ☐ Librarian ☐ Other *Notes/Comments*	☐ On site ☐ Remote Location
Set up a posting schedule	☐ Teens ☐ Librarian ☐ Other *Notes/Comments*	☐ On site ☐ Remote Location
Set up a responsibilities list	☐ Teens ☐ Librarian ☐ Other *Notes/Comments*	☐ On site ☐ Remote Location

Task	Who Is Responsible?	Where?
Design the blog look and feel	☐ Teens ☐ Librarian ☐ Other *Notes/Comments*	☐ On site ☐ Remote Location
Write blog entries	☐ Teens ☐ Librarian ☐ Other *Notes/Comments*	☐ On site ☐ Remote Location
Advertise the blog	☐ Teens ☐ Librarian ☐ Other *Notes/Comments*	☐ On site ☐ Remote Location
Evaluate the success of the blog	☐ Teens ☐ Librarian ☐ Other *Notes/Comments*	☐ On site ☐ Remote Location
Other	☐ Teens ☐ Librarian ☐ Other *Notes/Comments*	☐ On site ☐ Remote Location

After looking through the checklist, where would you put this youth participatory activity on the Ladder of Participation that is shown in figure 5-2?

IS TRAINING NECESSARY?

The teens' level of participation in this activity will determine the type of training and skill development needed. The following table outlines a few of the areas in which teens might need support.

Activity	Training/Skill Development Required
Develop weblog or software evaluation criteria	Evaluation skills
Install and configure weblog software on library server	Ability to upload and download files, knowledge of file and folder structure, and understanding of server side scripts
Design the blog look and feel	Understanding of graphic design principles and knowledge of HTML coding

THE BOTTOM LINE

Blogs are a communication tool that gives teens a chance to read, write, and evaluate. Blogging uses the capabilities of the Internet to great advantage and allows teens to express themselves in a format they feel comfortable with. Adults sometimes worry about the content in teen blogs, but if they are created as a part of a library youth participation activity librarians can help teens learn how to use the blog format appropriately.

FIGURE 5-2
Ladder of Participation

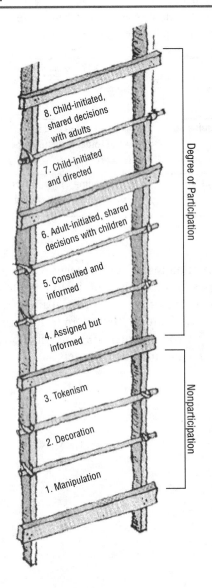

8. Child-initiated, shared decisions with adults

7. Child-initiated and directed

6. Adult-initiated, shared decisions with children

5. Consulted and informed

4. Assigned but informed

Degree of Participation

3. Tokenism

2. Decoration

1. Manipulation

Nonparticipation

Source: Roger Hart, *Children's Participation: From Tokenism to Citizenship.* Innocenti Essay no. 4 (Florence: UNICEF International Child Development Center, 1992).

Teen Guides

In this activity teens develop discussion guides for books, movies, websites, TV shows, and so on. The guides can be created with word processing software and made available in paper format or they can be posted on the web using HTML or web authoring software.

WHERE'S THE YOUTH PARTICIPATION?

Teens who participate in this activity might:

- Choose what books, movies, websites, TV shows, and so on, to create discussion guides for.
- Decide if the guides should be printed in paper format, posted on the web, or both.
- Read discussion guides available on the web and in paper to determine what works best.
- Develop evaluation criteria for discussion guides.
- Create discussion guide content.
- Design the guides either with word processing/desktop publishing software or for the web.
- Print or publish the guides on the web.
- Advertise and distribute the guides.
- Evaluate guide development process and content.

WHY WOULD TEENS WANT TO DO IT?

Teens who create the discussion guides become a community resource others can rely upon to develop programs and services. The activity gives them a chance to inform librarians about the types of discussions that appeal to their peers. As a result, they feel a sense of empowerment and are motivated to succeed.

HOW DOES IT SUPPORT ADOLESCENT LITERACY?

Earlier in this chapter the point was made that, by modeling expertise in a particular area while at the same time helping teens gain their own expertise in that area, librarians provide support to an adolescent's literacy development. Librarians can achieve that objective in a project like this by facilitating media discussions and helping teens understand when and why these discussions work or don't work. Teens can then use the information gleaned from the librarian, along with her knowledge of teen interests and communication preferences, to create useful guides.

WHAT DEVELOPMENTAL ASSETS DOES IT MEET?

See appendix A for more information on the development assets of adolescents.

Other adult relationships	Community values youth	Youth as resources
Service to others	Adults as role models	Positive peer influence
High expectations	Creative activities	Youth programs
Achievement motivation	Responsibility	Planning and decision making
Self-esteem	Sense of purpose	

WHO HAS THE RESPONSIBILITY?

The following checklist outlines the various tasks that need to be accomplished in order to carry out this activity. Use it to determine the level of participation teens will have, who will be responsible for the various steps in the process, and where each task needs to be accomplished. Some tasks might require checking more than one box.

Task	Who Is Responsible?	Where?
Decide to take on the project	☐ Teens ☐ Librarian ☐ Other *Notes/Comments*	☐ On site ☐ Remote Location
Select topics on which to create guides	☐ Teens ☐ Librarian ☐ Other *Notes/Comments*	☐ On site ☐ Remote Location

Task	Who Is Responsible?	Where?
Determine guide format—print, web, both	☐ Teens ☐ Librarian ☐ Other *Notes/Comments*	☐ On site ☐ Remote Location
Develop guide creation time-line	☐ Teens ☐ Librarian ☐ Other *Notes/Comments*	☐ On site ☐ Remote Location
Assign discussion guide responsibilities	☐ Teens ☐ Librarian ☐ Other *Notes/Comments*	☐ On site ☐ Remote Location
Evaluate other discussion guides	☐ Teens ☐ Librarian ☐ Other *Notes/Comments*	☐ On site ☐ Remote Location
Develop discussion guide criteria	☐ Teens ☐ Librarian ☐ Other *Notes/Comments*	☐ On site ☐ Remote Location
Create discussion guide content	☐ Teens ☐ Librarian ☐ Other *Notes/Comments*	☐ On site ☐ Remote Location

Task	Who Is Responsible?	Where?
Design guide in format previously determined	☐ Teens ☐ Librarian ☐ Other *Notes/Comments*	☐ On site ☐ Remote Location
Print/publish guides	☐ Teens ☐ Librarian ☐ Other *Notes/Comments*	☐ On site ☐ Remote Location
Advertise/distribute guides	☐ Teens ☐ Librarian ☐ Other *Notes/Comments*	☐ On site ☐ Remote Location
Evaluate guide content and success	☐ Teens ☐ Librarian ☐ Other *Notes/Comments*	☐ On site ☐ Remote Location
Other	☐ Teens ☐ Librarian ☐ Other *Notes/Comments*	☐ On site ☐ Remote Location

After looking through the checklist, where would you put this youth participatory activity on the Ladder of Participation that is shown in figure 5-3?

IS TRAINING NECESSARY?

The teens' level of participation in this activity will determine the type of training and skill development needed. The following table outlines a few of the areas in which teens might need support.

Activity	Training/Skill Development Required
Evaluate discussion guides	Assistance in locating guides and knowledge of evaluation skills.
Develop guide content	Writing workshop
Design and create guides in print or online format	Understanding of principles of graphic design and how they differ based on format; knowledge of word processing or publishing software; knowledge of HTML or web authoring software

THE BOTTOM LINE

A search of the literature on library discussion groups reveals that there are a wealth of articles on how to run a book discussion group, many of which include helpful hints on making a discussion group work with a particular audience. Publishers are well aware that discussion groups are a popular tool for librarians and teachers. Their websites often include discussion guides for the books they publish. Teens know what their peers are interested in talking about when it comes to books, movies, TV shows, and so on. Developing media discussion guides allows teens to create content that uses their expertise, that supports literacy development, and that serves a visible need of librarians and teachers.

BENEFITS OF LITERACY PROGRAMMING

This chapter explored the types of literacy support adolescents need and how technology-based youth participation activities in the library can provide that support. Literacy development doesn't end in elementary school. It's an ongoing process that can be enhanced through library activities, particularly technology-oriented activities that give teenagers a chance to participate meaningfully.

FIGURE 5-3
Ladder of Participation

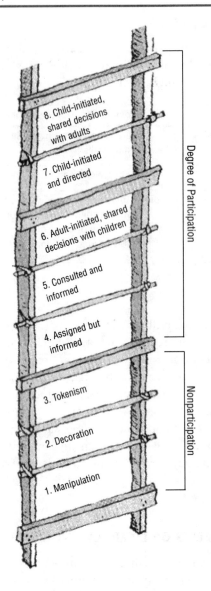

8. Child-initiated, shared decisions with adults

7. Child-initiated and directed

6. Adult-initiated, shared decisions with children

5. Consulted and informed

4. Assigned but informed

3. Tokenism

2. Decoration

1. Manipulation

Degree of Participation

Nonparticipation

Source: Roger Hart, *Children's Participation: From Tokenism to Citizenship.* Innocenti Essay no. 4 (Florence: UNICEF International Child Development Center, 1992).

When developing teen youth participatory activities in the library, remember that teens don't just need support on information, computer, or media literacy. Make sure the projects are just as strong in the acquisition of reading and writing skills. It will be worth the effort for the library, the teens, and the community.

NOTES

1. David W. Moore, Thomas W. Bean, Deanna Birdyshaw, and James A. Rycik. *Adolescent Literacy: A Position Statement for the Commission on Adolescent Literacy* (Washington, D.C.: International Reading Association, 1999). Summary available at http://www.ira.org/positions/adol_lit.html. Accessed 25 February 2003.
2. Ibid.
3. Ibid.
4. Ethel Himmel and William James Wilson, *Planning for Results: A Public Library Transformation Process* (Chicago: Public Library Association, 1998).
5. Young Adult Library Services Association and Patrick Jones, *New Directions for Library Service to Young Adults* (Chicago: ALA, 2002), 70–77.
6. Central Rappahannock Regional Library, "Web Surfers." Available at http://www.teenspoint.org/free_programs/web_surfers/index.asp. Accessed 25 February 2003.
7. Rebecca Purdy and the Web Surfers from Central Rappahannock Regional Library, "Introducing the Web Surfers' Review Code," *Voice of Youth Advocates* (October 2002): 262. Available at http://www.voya.com/WhatsInVoya/YAClicks.pdf. Accessed 25 February 2003.

CHAPTER 6

Getting Things Done at the Library

Picture this: It's after school, and the library is busy. Teens are working on projects and hanging out. Three middle school students walk over to the librarian's desk and ask, "Got anything for us to do?" The librarian says, "Yes I do. I need some leaves cut out of construction paper for story hour next week. Can you guys do that?" The teens agree to give it a try, the librarian sets them up with the task, and the leaves are made.

Does this scenario sound familiar? It should because some version of it goes on in libraries across the country weekly, if not daily. Often, teens come to the library to hang out, get a little bored, and think it wouldn't be a bad idea to see if the librarian had something for them to do. It's great that they are interested in helping, but what if there were an organized way for them to help, and what if the projects assigned had a strong connection to their lives and to the community?

As mentioned in chapter 2, volunteering, community service, and remuneration are three ways to connect with teens in a youth participatory fashion. Each has its place, and each might be used at different times and for different types of activities. Remember, teens need to be involved in meaningful activities; "busy work" doesn't cut it.

PUTTING A PROGRAM TOGETHER

Whether teens help out the library to earn community service credits, a salary, a stipend, or a combination of incentives, it's important to create a structure for their activity. Actually, it's essential to have a specific program in place so that teens who are interested in helping out have a framework within which to work. The Governor's Office on Service and Volunteerism for the state of Maryland published a paper titled "Best Practices for Developing a Volunteer Program" that identifies nine elements required to provide successful volunteer experiences.[1] While the document focuses on volunteering, the ideas also relate to community service and paid jobs in the library. The elements are:

- planning and organization
- policies and procedures
- recruitment
- screening, interviewing, and placement
- orientation and training
- supervision
- performance evaluation
- retention and recognition
- measuring program effectiveness

The aforementioned activities aren't much different from what needs to be accomplished when running any type of library program. However, within a youth participatory context some take on a slightly different light. The following discussion examines what the process might look like if teens were involved from the very beginning.

Planning and organization. Among the questions to consider when planning a youth participatory activity that focuses on working on library programs and services are:

- What are the jobs on which teens can work?
- How does the activity support the library's mission?
- How does the activity support adolescent development?

As a part of a youth participatory activity the teens should help you answer the first two questions. It's important to outline some possible library jobs for the teenagers and ask them to help you determine which are best suited to their skills and interests. It's a perfect opportunity to talk about the library's mission and how the jobs the teens might take on will support that mission.

Of course the discussion with teens about the different library-related work activities they might take on won't include specifics about how the work will help them develop successfully. However, as you discuss possibilities with the teens, keep in mind the forty developmental assets for adolescents (see appendix A) as well as information covered in earlier chapters of *Technically Involved.* Consider how the activities might be organized to meet the assets.

Policies and procedures. Don't forget to get teen input on this as well. Ask the teens if they think there should be different policies and procedures for each type of job they might do or if the library's general policies and procedures will provide an adequate framework for their activities. This is a good opportunity for the librarian to show teens some of the policies and procedures that the library already has in place related to technology. She can facilitate a discussion about why those rules exist, how they were developed, and the role of policies and procedures in the library. Ask teens if they think special guidelines might be needed for their projects. If teens determine the need for official library policies, make sure they have the opportunity to present the policies to the library's governing body for approval.

Recruitment. If this process began with teen involvement in the planning and policy making, it's likely that a core group of adolescents is ready to get to work. However, there might not be enough teens to perform all the tasks the teen planners decided to work on, and the library might want to keep certain jobs going after the first group of teens moves on. That means recruitment is a must. Work with the teens to develop a plan for getting the word out to their peers about the opportunities at the library. When working on technology-oriented library tasks, word of mouth might actually be a good way to start gathering more teens to the activity. Kimberly Bolan Taney at the Webster Public Library reports that many teens are interested in the library's page program, and a number of them learned about the job through word of mouth.[2]

Don't forget that the library and the teens can use outside resources for recruitment. Contacting other agencies in the community that might have connections to teenagers who fit the needs of the activity works well. Giving teens the chance to make those connections will help them gain important social skills and demonstrate to community members their involvement in positive projects.

Screening, interviewing, and placement. Even volunteers need to understand that the jobs they do are important and that good matches need to be made between specific skills and the jobs that need to be done. In a youth participation context, teens can compile a list of skills required for the different tasks and then develop a set of interview questions that will help the library and the teens decide who is best for which job or for a specific aspect of a particular job. Teens who are going to work with technology need to have requisite skills, while those who are going to work with the public need to be able to work well with people. In talking about the interviews she conducts, Kimberly Bolan Taney stated, "I'm really fussy when we go through the interview process. The customer service and technology connection is important. Teens need to have the right personality along with the right technology skills."[3]

Orientation and training. This isn't the first time this topic has come up in *Technically Involved.* Teens who are going to work on library projects need to have the skills necessary to complete those projects. Teens who have been involved in library youth participatory projects for a period of time are often called upon to train their peers on the tasks that need to be accomplished. Gina Macaluso at the Tucson Pima Public Library, where teens help patrons of all ages with computers, stated that teens need to be familiar with the library's approach to customer service and need to know when to turn something over to a librarian. Macaluso highlighted that librarians help teens distinguish between the librarian's role and the role of a tech. They know that when a job goes beyond pushing buttons it needs to be turned over to a librarian.[4]

At the Tucson Pima Library, teens who work with the computers keep a log book of the questions they were not able to answer when helping the public. The library staff uses the questions to develop further training for teen workers.

Supervision and performance evaluation. Maybe the teens are just helping out on a voluntary basis; maybe they are completing a community service requirement for school; or maybe they are paid employees of the library. No matter what the situation, it's important that teens helping out at the library realize that someone is paying attention to what they are doing and will provide feedback on their work. Chapter 5 discussed the importance of feedback to a teenager's literacy development. Feedback on the library tasks the teens are working on is just as important to their emotional and intellectual development. The teens should have the opportunity to develop their own assessment tools for evaluating the work they do.

LET THEM KNOW YOU CARE

Teen volunteers at the Mesa, Arizona, libraries attend the city volunteer luncheon. In talking about teen attendance at the luncheon, librarian Diane Tuccillo stated, "Teens get to see that they are a part of the adult community of volunteers."

Source: Phone interview with Diane Tuccillo, City of Mesa Library, December 13, 2002.

Retention and recognition. Everyone likes to know that a job was done well and is appreciated. Teens are no different. That means the library, with the help of the teens, needs to build in opportunities to demonstrate that what the teens are accomplishing is worthwhile. At the highest level of recognition, teens who participate in library work activities might get the chance to speak at national, state, or regional conferences. But it's not necessary to go to the highest level. Talk to the teens about what form of recognition they would like to get for their efforts. If a teen submits a website review online at the Central Rappahannock Regional Library and it's published in VOYA, the reviewer gets two free passes to the movies. That's a good form of recognition that probably spurs teens on to write reviews. Other libraries waive fines for teens involved in library work activities. Even if teens are being paid for the jobs they do or are getting community service or other type of credit, they will appreciate some other form of recognition.

In the technology construct teens might create a website or e-mail newsletter that highlights what they do and who they are. The New York Public Library (NYPL) has teen pages who help with computers during out-of-school hours. The NYPL's website has profiles of some of the computer pages and pictures of them at work.[5] Publicity like that is good for both teens and the library.

HOW TO DO IT:
TEMPLATES FOR YOUNG ADULT
LIBRARY PROJECTS

Teens volunteer because they think it's cool. They also think technology is cool, so the two together—working in the library and working with technology—are quite a powerful combination. Some library programs recognize this and use teens as volunteers and pages. Teens teach people how to use computers, troubleshoot computers, maintain computers, wire libraries, enter data into spreadsheets and databases, and more. The following youth participatory activity outlines suggest three technology-based activities teens can become involved in as a means of helping around the library. While it might not be possible to achieve the highest level of participation, as shown on the Ladder of Participation, the outlines should help you move to the top half of the ladder.

Wires No More

This activity gives teens the opportunity to research wireless technologies and make recommendations to the library administration about what approach they should take to integrate wireless into their facilities, programs, and services.

WHERE'S THE YOUTH PARTICIPATION?

Teens who participate in this activity might:

- Research topics related to wireless technologies, including standards, hardware, and software.
- Investigate the library's current and future technology needs.
- Test different wireless devices and/or visit locations using wireless devices to see how they work.
- Interview wireless users to learn about pros and cons of the technology in the library setting.
- Develop a list of uses for wireless technology in the library.
- Develop a set of criteria for determining what wireless products are best for the library.
- Design an implementation plan for the library's wireless technology.
- Develop a budget for the wireless implementation.
- Write a report of findings and recommendations.
- Design a presentation for the library administration about wireless findings and recommendations.
- Present the findings and recommendations to the library administration.
- Evaluate the process and the product.

WHY WOULD TEENS WANT TO DO IT?

A project like Wires No More gives teens a chance to be involved in important aspects of library decision making. The work they do and the recommendations they make will have an impact on the services the library provides. The ability to learn about a new technology "on the job," and to "play" with it before their friends can, really boosts a teen's self-esteem.

WHAT ARE SOME ELEMENTS OF PROGRAM EFFECTIVENESS?

In embarking on a project like Wires No More it is important to give teens a solid understanding of the role technology plays in the library and how technology supports the library's mission. Teens will have to carefully plan the steps they take in order to locate and evaluate information that will lead to a set of useful recommendations. Librarians have to make sure the teens involved in the project have a variety of skills. Some will need to understand the ins and outs of technology, while others will need good writing and communications skills. Once the project is complete it's important to spread the word about the work of the teens. This could be done in a number of ways, such as a special website that includes the group's findings and recommendations or articles in local newspapers.

WHAT DEVELOPMENTAL ASSETS DOES IT MEET?

See appendix A for more information on developmental assets for adolescents.

Other adult relationships	Community values youth	Youth as resources
Adult role models	Positive peer influence	High expectations
Creative activities	Youth programs	Achievement motivation
Responsibility	Planning and decision making	Interpersonal competence
Personal power	Self-esteem	Sense of purpose
Positive view of personal future		

WHO HAS THE RESPONSIBILITY?

The following checklist outlines the various tasks that need to be accomplished in order to carry out this activity. Use it to determine the level of participation teens will have, who will be responsible for the various steps in the process, and where each task needs to be accomplished. Some tasks might require checking more than one box.

Task	Who Is Responsible?	Where?
Decide to take on the project	☐ Teens ☐ Librarian ☐ Other *Notes/Comments*	☐ On site ☐ Remote Location

Task	Who Is Responsible?	Where?
Develop a project timeline	☐ Teens ☐ Librarian ☐ Other *Notes/Comments*	☐ On site ☐ Remote Location
Assign responsibilities	☐ Teens ☐ Librarian ☐ Other *Notes/Comments*	☐ On site ☐ Remote Location
Research wireless topics	☐ Teens ☐ Librarian ☐ Other *Notes/Comments*	☐ On site ☐ Remote Location
Investigate current and future uses of library technology	☐ Teens ☐ Librarian ☐ Other *Notes/Comments*	☐ On site ☐ Remote Location
Test wireless devices	☐ Teens ☐ Librarian ☐ Other *Notes/Comments*	☐ On site ☐ Remote Location
Take part in wireless site visits	☐ Teens ☐ Librarian ☐ Other *Notes/Comments*	☐ On site ☐ Remote Location

Task	Who Is Responsible?	Where?
Interview users of wirless	☐ Teens ☐ Librarian ☐ Other *Notes/Comments*	☐ On site ☐ Remote Location
Develop list of uses of wireless technology in the library	☐ Teens ☐ Librarian ☐ Other *Notes/Comments*	☐ On site ☐ Remote Location
Develop criteria for wireless evaluation	☐ Teens ☐ Librarian ☐ Other *Notes/Comments*	☐ On site ☐ Remote Location
Design an implementation plan	☐ Teens ☐ Librarian ☐ Other *Notes/Comments*	☐ On site ☐ Remote Location
Develop an implementation budget	☐ Teens ☐ Librarian ☐ Other *Notes/Comments*	☐ On site ☐ Remote Location
Write findings and recommendations report	☐ Teens ☐ Librarian ☐ Other *Notes/Comments*	☐ On site ☐ Remote Location

Task	Who Is Responsible?	Where?
Develop presentation on findings and recommendations	☐ Teens ☐ Librarian ☐ Other *Notes/Comments*	☐ On site ☐ Remote Location
Present findings and recommendations to library administration	☐ Teens ☐ Librarian ☐ Other *Notes/Comments*	☐ On site ☐ Remote Location
Other	☐ Teens ☐ Librarian ☐ Other *Notes/Comments*	☐ On site ☐ Remote Location

After looking through the checklist, where would you put this youth participatory activity on the Ladder of Participation that is shown in figure 6-1?

IS TRAINING NECESSARY?

The teens' level of participation in this activity will determine the type of training and skill development needed. The following table outlines a few of the areas in which teens might need support.

Activity	Training/Skill Development Required
Research wireless	Research skills
Evaluate wireless	Evaluation skills
Conduct interviews and site visits	Interviewing/communications skills
Develop presentation	PowerPoint (or other presentation software) skills
Present findings and recommendations	Public speaking skills

THE BOTTOM LINE

The library gives teens a high level of responsibility in a program that allows them to research, evaluate, select, and recommend how and why a certain technology should be integrated into the library's facilities, programs, and services. Of course, library staff would need to work with the teens along the way to help them understand the mission of the library and the impact their recommendations and findings might have on the library and the community. Perhaps different library staff members could work with the teens on different aspects of the project. Someone in the technology department might have skills that will prove useful at one point, while the young adult librarian's skills will prove useful at another. The more staff members the teens can interact with in a project like this the better.

FIGURE 6-1
Ladder of Participation

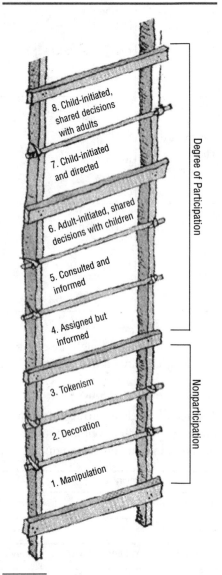

Source: Roger Hart, *Children's Participation: From Tokenism to Citizenship.* Innocenti Essay no. 4 (Florence: UNICEF International Child Development Center, 1992).

Online Tour Guides

Teen tour guides create web-based tours of the library that might include images, floor plans, staff information, and historical notes.

WHERE'S THE YOUTH PARTICIPATION?

Teens who participate in this activity might:

- Investigate online building tours for libraries, museums, and so on.
- Develop a set of criteria for evaluating online facilities tours.
- Take photos of the library or locate photos that can be scanned.
- Digitize photos either by importing with a digital camera or scanning.
- Use image editing software.
- Draw library floor plans.
- Interview staff about the library building.
- Research the history of the library building.
- Create the text that will accompany the web-based tour.
- Design the look and feel of the tour for the web.
- Code the website.
- Advertise the website.
- Maintain the website.
- Evaluate the website creation process and the final product.

WHY WOULD TEENS WANT TO DO IT?

Teens who take part in this activity will get a chance to see the behind-the-scenes workings of the library. While going behind the scenes might not in and of itself be exciting to teens, when it is combined with a specific job and responsibility it becomes more enticing. Teens who work on the online tour will act as a community resource and provide the library with a useful public relations tool.

WHAT ARE SOME ELEMENTS OF PROGRAM EFFECTIVENESS?

Even if the teens who work on this project have been library users for their entire lives, they will need a tour of the facilities in which the librarian points out areas they might not be aware of. Teens will need to understand what goes on behind the scenes in the various offices. They might have to be trained in photography techniques to get quality images and in the use of digital imaging software to enhance photos for the site. Teens will have to plan how the tour will be presented on the Web, paying careful attention to how the library's physical space can be successfully transferred to a virtual medium.

WHAT DEVELOPMENTAL ASSETS DOES IT MEET?

See appendix A for more information on developmental assets for adolescents.

Other adult relationships	Community values youth	Youth as resources
Adult role models	Positive peer influence	High expectations
Achievement motivation	Responsibility	Planning and decision making
Interpersonal competence	Personal power	Self-esteem
Sense of purpose		

WHO HAS THE RESPONSIBILITY?

The following checklist outlines the various tasks that need to be accomplished in order to carry out this activity. Use it to determine the level of participation teens will have, who will be responsible for the various steps in the process, and where each task needs to be accomplished. Some tasks might require checking more than one box.

Task	Who Is Responsible?	Where?
Decide to take on the project	☐ Teens ☐ Librarian ☐ Other *Notes/Comments*	☐ On site ☐ Remote Location
Develop a project timeline	☐ Teens ☐ Librarian ☐ Other *Notes/Comments*	☐ On site ☐ Remote Location

Task	Who Is Responsible?	Where?
Assign responsi-bilities	☐ Teens ☐ Librarian ☐ Other *Notes/Comments*	☐ On site ☐ Remote Location
Investigate online building tours	☐ Teens ☐ Librarian ☐ Other *Notes/Comments*	☐ On site ☐ Remote Location
Evaluate online facility tours	☐ Teens ☐ Librarian ☐ Other *Notes/Comments*	☐ On site ☐ Remote Location
Take photos	☐ Teens ☐ Librarian ☐ Other *Notes/Comments*	☐ On site ☐ Remote Location
Locate photos	☐ Teens ☐ Librarian ☐ Other *Notes/Comments*	☐ On site ☐ Remote Location
Scan or digitize photos	☐ Teens ☐ Librarian ☐ Other *Notes/Comments*	☐ On site ☐ Remote Location

Task	Who Is Responsible?	Where?
Use image editing software	☐ Teens ☐ Librarian ☐ Other *Notes/Comments*	☐ On site ☐ Remote Location
Draw floor plans	☐ Teens ☐ Librarian ☐ Other *Notes/Comments*	☐ On site ☐ Remote Location
Interview library staff	☐ Teens ☐ Librarian ☐ Other *Notes/Comments*	☐ On site ☐ Remote Location
Research library building history	☐ Teens ☐ Librarian ☐ Other *Notes/Comments*	☐ On site ☐ Remote Location
Write tour content	☐ Teens ☐ Librarian ☐ Other *Notes/Comments*	☐ On site ☐ Remote Location
Design the tour	☐ Teens ☐ Librarian ☐ Other *Notes/Comments*	☐ On site ☐ Remote Location

Task	Who Is Responsible?	Where?
Code the web pages	☐ Teens ☐ Librarian ☐ Other *Notes/Comments*	☐ On site ☐ Remote Location
Maintain the website	☐ Teens ☐ Librarian ☐ Other *Notes/Comments*	☐ On site ☐ Remote Location
Advertise the website	☐ Teens ☐ Librarian ☐ Other *Notes/Comments*	☐ On site ☐ Remote Location
Evaluate the site and the process	☐ Teens ☐ Librarian ☐ Other *Notes/Comments*	☐ On site ☐ Remote Location
Other	☐ Teens ☐ Librarian ☐ Other *Notes/Comments*	☐ On site ☐ Remote Location

After looking through the checklist, where would you put this youth participatory activity on the Ladder of Participation that is shown in figure 6-2?

IS TRAINING NECESSARY?

The teens' level of participation in this activity will determine the type of training and skill development needed. The following table outlines a few of the areas in which teens might need support.

Activity	Training/Skill Development Required
Investigate online building tours	Research skills
Develop facility tour evaluation criteria	Evaluation skills
Take photos	Photography principles
Digitize photos	Use of a scanner or ability to import photos from a digital camera to a computer
Edit photos	Ability to use image editing software such as Paint Shop Pro, Photoshop, Image Ready, or Photoshop Elements
Research library building history	Research skills including use and location of primary source documents
Interview staff	Communications and interviewing skills
Design the site	Knowledge of web design principles, graphic design, or image editing/creation software
Code the site	Knowledge of HTML or web creation software. Knowledge of file and folder structure and the ability to upload and download files

FIGURE 6-2
Ladder of Participation

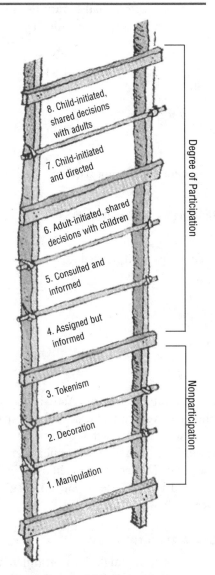

8. Child-initiated, shared decisions with adults

7. Child-initiated and directed

6. Adult-initiated, shared decisions with children

5. Consulted and informed

4. Assigned but informed

Degree of Participation

3. Tokenism

2. Decoration

1. Manipulation

Nonparticipation

Source: Roger Hart, *Children's Participation: From Tokenism to Citizenship.* Innocenti Essay no. 4 (Florence: UNICEF International Child Development Center, 1992).

THE BOTTOM LINE

Ever find a teen in a part of the library where he wasn't supposed to be? Teens often try to see how far they can go before getting into trouble, and one way they do that in libraries is to go into staff offices, work rooms, and other areas that are off-limits. Why not turn that mischievous interest into a project that works to the library's benefit? Teens who develop web-based tours will get to see what goes on in the library, and perhaps the people who work there, from a different perspective. They will feel empowered by creating something the world will be able to see on the web. Some will advance their technology skills by learning new hardware or software.

The Ins and Outs of E-Mail Newsletters

The teens who participate in this activity will create e-mail library newsletters highlighting library events and information for a specific audience.

WHERE'S THE YOUTH PARTICIPATION?

Teens who participate in this activity might:

- Decide the audiences on which to focus.
- Determine publication schedule.
- Design a subscription form.
- Gather e-mail addresses (if subscription form is not used).
- Investigate bulk e-mail options.
- Develop criteria to evaluate bulk e-mail software if needed.
- Evaluate bulk e-mail software if needed.
- Raise funds to purchase bulk e-mail software if needed.
- Gather library news and information.
- Write the newsletter.
- Distribute the newsletter via e-mail.
- Advertise the availability of the newsletter.

WHY WOULD TEENS WANT TO DO IT?

Who would want to spend time writing about the library? Actually, some teens would. Think about the teens who get involved in the school newspaper and the yearbook. What is it about those activities that attracts them? Something to put on a college application? Yes, but they also offer them a chance to try out a different format for writing. The teens get to choose what's included, how it's organized, and how it will look. These opportunities give teens a sense of purpose and importance to their community.

WHAT ARE SOME ELEMENTS OF PROGRAM EFFECTIVENESS?

Certainly every project takes planning, but this one might be a bit different from the ones teens are regularly involved in. As a part of the e-mail newsletter project teens will have to plan the contents of the newsletter based on the target audience. If writing for adults, teens will need to consider the language they use in order to get the information across appropriately to that population. If writing for children, the writing style and format would have to meet that population's needs. As teens decide what audiences they want to work with, it is important for them to consider the differences between the audiences. The librarian can play a pivotal role in helping teens understand how the library serves different age groups differently.

This activity might continue for several years, so the teens and librarian should come up with a plan to ensure that there are always teens in the community who are interested in participating.

WHAT DEVELOPMENTAL ASSETS DOES IT MEET?

See appendix A for more information on the developmental assets for adolescents.

Other adult relationships	Community values youth	Youth as resources
Service to others	High expectations	Creative activities
Youth programs	Responsibility	Planning and decision making
Personal power	Self-esteem	

WHO HAS THE RESPONSIBILITY?

The following checklist outlines the various tasks that need to be accomplished in order to carry out this activity. Use it to determine the level of participation teens will have, who will be responsible for the various steps in the process, and where each task needs to be accomplished. Some tasks might require checking more than one box.

Task	Who Is Responsible?	Where?
Decide to take on the project	☐ Teens ☐ Librarian ☐ Other *Notes/Comments*	☐ On site ☐ Remote Location

Task	Who Is Responsible?	Where?
Decide newsletter audience	☐ Teens ☐ Librarian ☐ Other *Notes/Comments*	☐ On site ☐ Remote Location
Design subscription form	☐ Teens ☐ Librarian ☐ Other *Notes/Comments*	☐ On site ☐ Remote Location
Gather e-mail addresses	☐ Teens ☐ Librarian ☐ Other *Notes/Comments*	☐ On site ☐ Remote Location
Investigate bulk e-mail options	☐ Teens ☐ Librarian ☐ Other *Notes/Comments*	☐ On site ☐ Remote Location
Develop criteria to evaluate bulk e-mail software if needed	☐ Teens ☐ Librarian ☐ Other *Notes/Comments*	☐ On site ☐ Remote Location
Evaluate bulk e-mail software if needed	☐ Teens ☐ Librarian ☐ Other *Notes/Comments*	☐ On site ☐ Remote Location

Task	Who Is Responsible?	Where?
Raise funds to purchase bulk e-mail software if needed	☐ Teens ☐ Librarian ☐ Other *Notes/Comments*	☐ On site ☐ Remote Location
Determine publication schedule	☐ Teens ☐ Librarian ☐ Other *Notes/Comments*	☐ On site ☐ Remote Location
Gather newsletter information	☐ Teens ☐ Librarian ☐ Other *Notes/Comments*	☐ On site ☐ Remote Location
Write the newsletter	☐ Teens ☐ Librarian ☐ Other *Notes/Comments*	☐ On site ☐ Remote Location
Distribute the newsletter	☐ Teens ☐ Librarian ☐ Other *Notes/Comments*	☐ On site ☐ Remote Location
Advertise the newsletter	☐ Teens ☐ Librarian ☐ Other *Notes/Comments*	☐ On site ☐ Remote Location

Task	Who Is Responsible?	Where?
Evaluate the newsletter—process and product	☐ Teens ☐ Librarian ☐ Other *Notes/Comments*	☐ On site ☐ Remote Location
Other	☐ Teens ☐ Librarian ☐ Other *Notes/Comments*	☐ On site ☐ Remote Location

After looking through the checklist, where would you put this youth participatory activity on the Ladder of Participation that is shown in figure 6-3?

IS TRAINING NECESSARY?

The teens' level of participation in this activity will determine the type of training and skill development needed. The table below outlines a few of the areas in which teens might need support.

Activity	Training/Skill Development Required
Investigate bulk e-mail options	Research skills, understanding of bulk e-mail concepts
Develop bulk e-mail software criteria	Evaluation skills
Evaluate bulk e-mail software	Evaluation skills
Write e-mail content	Written communication skills

FIGURE 6-3
Ladder of Participation

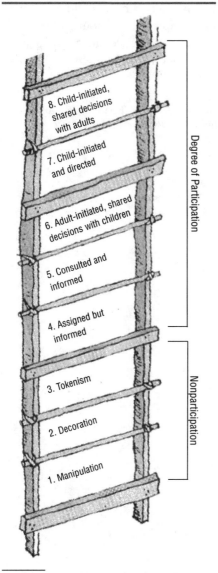

8. Child-initiated, shared decisions with adults

7. Child-initiated and directed

6. Adult-initiated, shared decisions with children

5. Consulted and informed

4. Assigned but informed

3. Tokenism

2. Decoration

1. Manipulation

Degree of Participation

Nonparticipation

Source: Roger Hart, *Children's Participation: From Tokenism to Citizenship.* Innocenti Essay no. 4 (Florence: UNICEF International Child Development Center, 1992).

THE BOTTOM LINE

Teens use e-mail regularly to communicate with peers, teachers, and family members, so they are familiar with the technology as it fits into their daily lives. They might not, however, have thought about how e-mail can be used as a marketing tool. While this activity uses bulk e-mail in a positive fashion, it can also provide opportunities to discuss unwanted bulk e-mail teens, their friends, and family members might receive. Teens can include their names on the e-mail newsletter so members of the community will know who is responsible for the material in their mailbox, and they will feel a sense of power in making decisions about what does and doesn't go into the newsletter. It might seem like an old-fashioned idea—using e-mail to inform a community about library news and events—but it can be a powerful tool for both the library and for a teen's development.

BENEFITS OF YOUNG ADULT LIBRARY PROJECTS

Think about the tasks teens in the library participate in regularly. Do they cut out shapes for story hour? Of course this task needs to be accomplished, but is it the best way to use the teens' skills and to help meet their developmental needs? Consider if there is a way to change that activity to include technology, to take on a youth participatory approach, and to provide more value to the teens and the library. Perhaps instead of cutting out shapes for story hour the teens can meet with the children's librarian to brainstorm activities children might do during story hour and then use word processing and image editing software to create accompanying materials for the children and the librarian. A new approach just might do the trick.

NOTES

1. Maryland Governor's Office on Service and Volunteerism, "Best Practices for Developing a Volunteer Program. Available at http://www.gov.state.md.us/pubs/bestprac/sec00.htm. Accessed 25 February 2003.
2. Kimberly Bolan Taney, telephone conversation, August 19, 2002.
3. Ibid.
4. Gina Macaluso, telephone conversation. August 15, 2002.
5. New York Public Library, "Computer Page Profiles: Success Stories." Available at http://www.nypl.org/branch/ref/pages/profiles.htm. Accessed 25 February 2003.

CHAPTER 7

Overcoming Obstacles

Up to this point, *Technically Involved* has covered the youth development and youth participation framework, techniques for getting teens involved in library activities, and examples of different technology-based youth participatory activities libraries might develop with teens. This last chapter looks at a few barriers (mentioned in chapter 2) librarians might face in getting youth participatory activities up and running, particularly when technology is added to the mix, and suggests ways to break down those barriers.

LIBRARY STAFF

One of the biggest barriers a librarian might face in trying to get teens involved in participatory activities is library staff. Staff members might not understand why such activities are important to adolescent development. To overcome the resistance, a librarian must educate coworkers about teen developmental assets and needs and the important role participation plays in a teen's successful growth.

Gina Macaluso of the Tucson Pima Public Library states, "Staff training on how to work with youth is the most important aspect of successful youth participation."[1] As a part of the Public Libraries as Partners in Youth Development (PLPYD) project sponsored by the Urban Libraries Council with funding from the DeWitt–Wallace Foundation, the Tucson Pima Public Library provided youth development training to staff members. After the project got going, the staff attended a half-day session in which a teen panel answered questions about their expectations of the library and their library experiences, good and bad. "Teens were very verbal," Macaluso notes. "Once they got going, there was no stopping them."[2]

What a great way to get teens involved in the staff training process. Teens in the Tucson Pima projects speak at local, regional, and national conferences. This not only gives them a chance to shine and feel an important part of their community, but it also gives librarians from outside the community an opportunity to see how teens can excel. That might be one of the best ways to dispel stereotypes.

WHERE TO FIND HELP

You don't have to start a youth participatory program on your own. YALSA has a cadre of Serving the Underserved (SUS) trainers who help library staff understand issues related to youth development and youth participation. Consult the YALSA website to find out who is available in your area.[3]

Another option is to work with agencies in the community that have expertise in issues related to youth development. Maybe there is an agency with a good computer lab that teens can use on a regular basis. Or maybe there is one with a technical specialist who can explain how technology works and would be a good mentor to the teens. If community agencies participate in the project, the result won't be just that library staff become more aware of teen needs and issues, but also that the larger community becomes more aware of the library and what it's trying to do for teens. Partnerships can be built and strengthened through technology-based youth participation activities sponsored at the library.

STAFF TRAINING TOPICS

The facts about youth development

The facts about adolescent developmental assets

The impact of youth participation on a teenager's life

The how and why of working with community agencies

The reasons behind teen interest in all things technological

Elaine Meyers, children's and youth manager of the Phoenix Public Library, reports that in Fort Bend, Texas, a library involved in a PLPYD project worked with community partners and set up labs in partner facilities. "To provide support, they had the kids wire the facilities. They taught them how to do sophisticated wiring and how to build their own computers."[4] Fort Bend didn't have to do it alone, and neither does any other library.

WHAT ABOUT THE IT DEPARTMENT?

Meyers also noted that "the IT department loved the project."[5] Most librarians, however, struggle to gain support not only from other librarians on staff, but also from the library's technology staff. How can you overcome this obstacle?

First, the technology personnel at the library *must* be included in the process from the very beginning. Maybe teens come up with the idea to work on a wireless project, but before they go any further than the idea stage it's the librarian's job to get the technology staff on board.

Actually, the first step is to talk to the technology people even before the teens have discussed technology-oriented youth participation activities. Explain that some of the projects will probably have a technology component. Find out if the IT people have any ideas for projects that might work well with teens and if anyone wants to talk with them about what's possible. Get the lay of the land to anticipate any resistance.

WHOM TO WORK WITH
Schools
Youth commissions
Hospitals
Police
Service organizations
Summer job programs
Recreation commissions
YMCA/YWCA
4-H
United Way

Keep the technology staff informed every step of the way. The best way to do this would be to hold joint meetings of teens and technology personnel. If that's not possible, make sure to immediately notify the IT department of any decisions the teens make that relate to the library's technology or that might require the technology staff's participation.

Of course, the library's technology staff should be included in the youth development and youth participation training. They need to understand as much as anyone else why the proposed projects are good for teens and the library. At the same time, they need to confront their stereotypes about teens. Perhaps there is a preconception that all the teens are going to do is visit porn sites or hack into the library's system and destroy it. Those preconceptions have to be dissolved.

If facing technology staff fears about teen interaction with technology, give the teens and the technology people an opportunity to talk to each other. Let the teens stick up for themselves and educate the technicians about who they really are. Before the meeting it would be a good idea to give the teens an idea of what needs to be discussed and what they might say in order to assuage any fears. But the day of the meeting let the teens take charge to show what they can do and who they can be.

Sometimes the library's technology support people work off-site. This can make it even harder to get the necessary points across, but the same techniques still apply. Ask the technology staff, even if they are from an outside agency or business, to attend meetings to learn about youth development and youth participation. Invite them to come to a meeting to hear what the teens have to say. If the staff works outside the library, a library administrator might have to talk to another agency's administration to get the ball rolling.

Why did the IT department love the Fort Bend experience? And why is it that Elaine Meyers could tell the story of a teen girl who used the stipend she received from the library as a part of the PLPYD project to buy computer parts and then went to the library's IT department for help when she needed it? The girl obviously felt comfortable with the IT department, and the department staff felt comfortable with teenagers. They built a rapport by working together on projects and saw that each had something of value to give to the community. When that happened, teenagers and technologists respected and valued each others skills and knowledge.

YOUTH PARTICIPATION AND TECHNOLOGY

Chapter 1 discussed why librarians should consider including technology in youth participation activities. That discussion looked at technology's role in youth development and examined how technology is a means to include teens who might not otherwise choose to participate in library activities.

When you add technology to youth participation it means the library is taking on a new level of commitment to the adolescents in the community. It means the library decided to accept teen interests and skills that are not simply related to reading, books, homework, and research. A library that integrates technology into youth participation says, "OK, we know there are teens out there who have a lot to give to the community. We also know that these teens might have interests we haven't thought much about before. But now we are ready."

Gina Macaluso, reflecting on the Tucson experience, said it best: "The most important outcome is that you are helping to change the face of the community and giving teens a chance to become productive adults."[6]

NOTES

1. Gina Macaluso, telephone conversation, August 15, 2002.
2. Ibid.
3. Young Adult Library Services Association, "SUS Trainers by State," 2003. Available at http://www.ala.org/yalsa/. Accessed 25 February 2003.
4. Elaine Meyers, telephone conversation, August 13, 2002.
5. Ibid.
6. Gina Macaluso.

Forty Developmental Assets
for Adolescents

CATEGORY	ASSET NAME AND DEFINITION

<table>
<tr><td rowspan="3">EXTERNAL ASSETS</td><td>Support</td><td>1. Family Support—Family life provides high levels of love and support.
2. Positive Family Communication—Young person and her or his parent(s) communicate positively, and young person is willing to seek advice and counsel from parents.
3. Other Adult Relationships—Young person receives support from three or more nonparent adults.
4. Caring Neighborhood—Young person experiences caring neighbors.
5. Caring School Climate—School provides a caring, encouraging environment.
6. Parent Involvement in Schooling—Parent(s) are actively involved in helping young person succeed in school.</td></tr>
<tr><td>Empowerment</td><td>7. Community Values Youth—Young person perceives that adults in the community value youth.
8. Youth as Resources—Young people are given useful roles in the community
9. Service to Others—Young person serves in the community one hour or more per week.
10. Safety—Young person feels safe at home, school, and in the neighborhood.</td></tr>
<tr><td>Boundaries & Expectations</td><td>11. Family Boundaries—Family has clear rules and consequences and monitors the young person's whereabouts.
12. School Boundaries—School provides clear rules and consequences.
13. Neighborhood Boundaries—Neighbors take responsibility for monitoring young people's behavior.
14. Adult Role Models—Parent(s) and other adults model positive responsible behavior.
15. Positive Peer Influence—Young person's best friends model responsible behavior.
16. High Expectations—Both parent(s) and teachers encourage the young person to do well.</td></tr>
</table>

	CATEGORY	ASSET NAME AND DEFINITION
EXTERNAL ASSETS	**Constructive Use of Time**	17. *Creative Activities*—Young person spends three or more hours per week in lessons or practice in music, theatre, or other arts. 18. *Youth Programs*—Young person spends three or more hours per week in sports, clubs, or organizations at school and/or in the community. 19. *Religious Community*—Young person spends one or more hours per week in activities in a religious institution 20. *Time at Home*—Young person is out with friends "with nothing special to do" two or fewer nights per week.
INTERNAL ASSETS	**Commitment to Learning**	21. *Achievement Motivation*—Young person is motivated to do well in school. 22. *School Engagement*—Young person is actively engaged in learning. 23. *Homework*—Young person reports doing at least one hour of homework every school day. 24. *Bonding to School*—Young person cares about her or his school. 25. *Reading for Pleasure*—Young person reads for pleasure three or more hours per week.
	Positive Values	26. *Caring*—Young person places high value on helping other people. 27. *Equality and Social Justice*—Young person places high value on promoting equality and reducing hunger and poverty. 28. *Integrity*—Young person acts on convictions and stands up for her or his beliefs. 29. *Honesty*—Young person "tells the truth even when it is not easy." 30. *Responsibility*—Young person accepts and takes responsibility. 31. *Restraint*—Young person believes it is important not to be sexually active or to use alcohol or other drugs.
	Social Competencies	32. *Planning and Decision Making*—Young person knows how to plan ahead and make choices. 33. *Interpersonal Competence*—Young person has empathy, sensitivity, and friendship skills. 34. *Cultural Competence*—Young person has knowledge of and comfort with people of different cultural/racial/ethnic backgrounds. 35. *Resistance Skills*—Young person can resist negative peer pressure and dangerous situations. 36. *Peaceful Conflict Resolution*—Young person seeks to resolve conflict nonviolently.

	CATEGORY	ASSET NAME AND DEFINITION
INTERNAL ASSETS	**Positive Identity**	37. *Personal Power*—Young person feels he or she has control over "things that happen to me." 38. *Self-Esteem*—Young person reports having a high self-esteem. 39. *Sense of Purpose*—Young person reports that "my life has a purpose." 40. *Positive View of Personal Future*—Young person is optimistic about her or his personal future.

Source: Search Institute, 615 First Ave., NE, Suite 125, Minneapolis, MN 55413, http://www.searchinstitute.org. Reprinted with permission.

National Youth Participation Guidelines

DEFINITION

Involvement of young adults, ages 12 through 18, in responsible action and significant services for their peers and the community.

INTRODUCTION

Although the concept of youth participation is neither foreign nor new, the Young Adult Library Services Association (YALSA) recognizes the need for a framework to facilitate the process of having young adults, ages twelve through eighteen, participate in any American Library Association activities at the national level.

Each committee or program chair is responsible for assessing the potential for the involvement of young adults, setting parameters for participation that specify objectives and outcomes and providing a balance between committee and young adult input. Neither committee decisions nor program content will be made based solely on young adult input but through a combination of professional knowledge and youth participation.

PURPOSE

To solicit the input of young adults and promote their participation in the creation and development of library activities, programs and publications, thus insuring the relevance of these products and services to the population we serve.

GOALS

To organize and implement youth participation to support division and committee goals,

To collect a wide range of ideas from as diverse a young adult population as possible,

To create valuable experiences for the participating young adults in which they can gain knowledge and/or skills useful in future endeavors,

To find opportunities for collaboration with other organizations that foster youth leadership.

PROCEDURES

Conference participation

Identification of youth participation groups near conference sites: The Youth Participation Coordinator will make available to any ALA committee a list of local contacts six months prior to the event. Committees and programs are urged to draw from more than one group and to seek diverse input.

Requests to attend: Invitations to attend a committee meeting or participate in programs or other events will be extended by the committee chair.

Registration: Committee or program chairs should make name badges for young adults attending their programs, and send requests to the YALSA Office for guest exhibitor passes.

Conference expenses: Any expense relating to conference attendance is the responsibility of the youth participant, unless other arrangements have been approved by the division or unit.

Evaluation: As a part of the evaluation for programs and committee activities, chairs will assess the impact of youth participation in a report to the Youth Participation Coordinator.

POTENTIAL ACTIVITIES

Creation of a YALSA teen advisory board

Creation of an interactive Internet feature where teens can share ideas with each other and with librarians

Training for youth as advocates for library services

Development of materials to recruit for and inform about the library profession

Observation of youth participation programs in conference city tours

Involvement of local teens in planning and/or staffing exhibit booths

Involvement of teens on the local arrangements committee

Involvement of teens in evaluating the market potential of library promotional materials

Consideration of teens as presenters and participants in YALSA programs

Approved by the YALSA Board of Directors, July 1997. Revised June 2001.

SOURCE: YALSA. Reprinted with permission.

The Impact of Youth Service

Youth service saves money

Teenagers volunteer 2.4 billion hours annually—worth $ 34.3 billion to the U.S. economy (Independent Sector/Gallup, 1996, and 1999 hourly value).

Tens of millions of dollars worth of service is carried out on National Youth Service Day alone

The value of service carried out on National Youth Service Day exceeds $171 million (Youth Service America estimates based on Independent Sector value of service, 1999).

Youth who volunteer do well in school

Youth who volunteer are more likely to do well in school, graduate, vote, and be philanthropic. (UCLA/Higher Education Research Institute, 1991).

Youth who volunteer are less likely to abuse alcohol and drugs

Youth who volunteer just one hour or more a week are 50 percent less likely to abuse drugs, alcohol, cigarettes, or engage in other destructive behavior (Search Institute, 1995).

Most Americans who donate time in their youth donate money in adulthood

81% of Americans who have volunteer experiences when they are young give to charitable organizations as adults (Independent Sector/Gallup, 1996).

Youth volunteering makes adult service more likely

Youth service makes adult volunteering three times more likely, creating a critical pipeline. Youth and adult service is worth $210 billion to the U.S. economy (Independent Sector/Gallup, 1996).

Volunteering helps teens develop leadership skills

Teens say the benefits received from volunteering are: Learning to respect others; learning to be helpful and kind; learning to understand people who are different from them; developing leadership skills, becoming more patient, and better understanding of good citizenship (Independent Sector/Gallup, 1996).

Source: Youth Service America, http://www.ysa.org. Reprinted with permission.

Trends in Youth Service

Service learning

There is an increased focus on schools or school/community partnerships which use service as a key educational tool to enhance learning as well as youth development. The number of high school students involved in service learning increased 3,663 percent.

Mandatory service

The number of school districts with community service requirements for students has doubled over the past decade to 30 percent. These programs, however, often lack administrative support.

Civic education

Across the country in schools, nonprofits, think tanks, and Congress, growing importance is being given to civic and character education and the vital role of service in this type of education and in strengthening civil society.

Civic engagement

Linked to the previous trend is the growing research on the lack of interest by young people in civic/political/policy aspects of their community. Organizations such as Do Something and ServiceVote 2000 demonstrate the disconnection between service and other political participation.

Positive youth development

Service is increasingly being utilized as one of the more effective strategies of general youth development programs. This trend responds to a growing body of evidence that shows that service increases youth and community "assets" (self-esteem, educational achievement, community infrastructure and services) while simultaneously reducing negative behaviors (drugs, violence, and teen sex).

Paid full-time service

There is a growing acceptance and understanding of paid service through programs such as AmeriCorps.

After-school, summertime, and international service programs

There is an increase in the number of summer and after-school service programs run mainly by nonprofits. There is also an increasing number of young Americans (10,000) participating in international service programs such as Peace Corps, Amigos de las Americas, and 150 other programs.

Involvement of younger children

Programs are targeting younger children in service learning and other service programs. This has been demonstrated by organizations such as Learn and Serve and PSSA that target children K–12.

Focus more on the impact/outcome of service done

Many funders are demanding more evaluation of the impact of service programs on beneficiaries and their communities.

More genuine youth participation rather than tokenism

Youth programs are developing better means to incorporate genuine youth participation in planning, implementing, and evaluating service programs.

Increased professionalism of the field

Programs are becoming more professional in terms of their administration, marketing, and implementation, but not necessarily evaluation.

Technology and access to information

Access to technology is increasing information on how, where, and why to volunteer, as well as increasing online recruiting of volunteers and sharing of best practices and other resources such as SERVEnet.org, Idealist.org, etc.

Research

Research on the impact, effectiveness, and scale of service programs is slowly increasing (Corporation for National Service, Independent Sector, Pew, etc.), although it is often questioned in terms of its accuracy and/or its tie to government evaluation of CNS programs.

SOURCE: Youth Service America, http://www.ysa.org. Reprinted with permission.

Youth Participation Technology Checklist

Use this checklist with teens to make sure all of the technology pieces are in place for youth participation activities.

Hardware Requirements

What do you need?

☐ Computers for project development

☐ Computers in private areas—not on the main floor of the library

☐ Computers to use with patrons, if so, how many _____

☐ Computer microphone   ☐ Computer speakers

☐ Scanner   ☐ Digital camera   ☐ Digital video camera   ☐ Color printer

☐ B&W printer

☐ Projection system—to hook the computer up for display on a screen

☐ Other _____

Does this project require an Internet connection at least some of the time?

☐ Yes   ☐ No

Software Requirements

What do you need?

☐ Word processing

☐ Spreadsheet

☐ Database

☐ Image creation/editing

☐ Web page creation

☐ Interactive media (e.g., Flash)

☐ Audio/Video (e.g., Real Player)

☐ Web browser

☐ FTP

☐ Weblog

☐ Discussion board

☐ E-mail

☐ Other _____

Partners

Library Staff

☐ Teen librarian

☐ Children's librarian

☐ Reference librarian

☐ Technical services

☐ Technology coordinator/staff

☐ Administrator(s), whom _____

☐ Circulation

☐ Other _____

Community Organizations/Agencies

List the organizations and agencies that might be good partners for getting this activity off the ground._____
_____
_____
_____

Can you work on this project outside of the library?   ☐ Yes   ☐ No

If yes, where else can you work on the project?

☐ Home   ☐ Classroom   ☐ Friend's house

☐ Other town building (e.g., youth center, YMCA, etc.)

☐ Other_____

If working on this project away from the library, what technology does the site you'll be using need?

Hardware

_____
_____
_____

Software

_____
_____
_____

Internet connection   ☐ Yes   ☐ No

Sample Volunteer Form

Consider using this type of form for youth participation activities that will include a technology component.

The Basics

Name _____

Address _____

Phone _____

E-mail _____

Grade _____

Age _____

School _____

In case of emergency, contact

Name _____

Home Phone _____

Work Phone _____

Name of Parent/Guardian _____

Parent/Guardian Signature _____

What are your two favorite things to do on the computer (e.g., make web pages, create/edit images, play games, download audio/video, watch movies, make movies, etc.)? _____

_____

_____

Have you ever taught someone else how to use a computer? ☐ Yes ☐ No

If you have, whom did you teach and what? _____

_____

_____

How would you like to help out with technology in the library?

☐ Troubleshoot computers   ☐ Teach people how to use the computers

☐ Make web pages   ☐ Take pictures

☐ Other _____

Self-Assessment Tool
for Youth/Adult Partnerships

This is not a test! Rate yourself on a scale from 1 to 5, with 1 being a beginner in this area. In the first column, indicate where you see yourself now. In the second column, indicate where you would like to be.

Where I am now:	Where I would like to be:	
_____	_____	Familiar with resources about youth participation and youth and adult partnerships (e.g., technical assistance, books, etc.).
_____	_____	Affirm and support people's feelings and ideas.
_____	_____	Treat all group members with respect.
_____	_____	Appreciate and incorporate the strength of similarities and differences among people (gender, spiritual, class, etc.).
_____	_____	Resist the urge to take over.
_____	_____	Careful about interrupting people of all ages.
_____	_____	Provide opportunities to have youth reflect and learn.
_____	_____	Believe in the potential and empowerment of all youth.
_____	_____	Trust youth to be powerful.
_____	_____	Be able to identify positive possibilities in difficult situations.
_____	_____	Listen carefully to people of all ages.
_____	_____	Get involved and provide support when a person puts down or devalues another or her/himself.

Where I am now:	Where I would like to be:	
_____	_____	Seek to learn from people.
_____	_____	Expect youth to make their own decisions.
_____	_____	Say something where young people's rights and due respect are being denied or violated.
_____	_____	Celebrate people's successes.
_____	_____	Advocate for improvement of youth/adult partnerships in teams, organizations, and communities.

Source: Innovation Center for Community and Youth Development, 7100 Connecticut Ave., Chevy Chase, MD 20815, http://www.theinnovationcenter.org. Reprinted with permission.

Software Tools

Below are suggestions for software tools to help you get started with a variety of youth participation activities in the library. This is not a comprehensive list; it merely provides jumping-off points.

WEBLOGS

Blogger.com. This site offers both free and pay options that allow users to create a blog and host it at Blogger.com or on the library's server. Available at http://www.blogger.com.

Greymatter. This free blogging software is downloadable and ready to be configured for the library's server. Available at http://www.noahgrey.com/greysoft.

Live Journal. This blogging site is no longer free, unless the user is referred by someone who already has a blog on the site. Available at http://www.livejournal.com.

Moveable Type. This highly customizable free blogging software can be downloaded to a computer and then configured for the library's server. Available at http://movabletype.org.

CHAT

DigiChat. This customizable chat software allows for creation of multiple rooms, password protecting rooms, and more. Available at http://www.digichat.com.

MultiCity. Another resource for creating customizable chat rooms with a full set of features. Available at http://www.multicity.com.

ParaChat. Offers both free and for-fee chat space that can either be hosted by ParaChat or the organization sponsoring the chat room. Available at http://www.parachat.com.

Yahoo! Chat. Yahoo! provides free chat space to those registered with the site. The chat room is available as long as there is at least one person in the room. Available at http://chat.yahoo.com.

IMAGE EDITING/CREATION

Adobe Elements, Image Ready, and Photoshop. Adobe Photoshop is the state-of-the-art image editing software in the web design world. Image Ready is specifically for creating images, including animated images, for the web. Adobe Elements is the company's lite version of the Photoshop software. Available at http://www.adobe.com.

Fireworks. This image editing program from Macromedia is available as an integrated element with Dreamweaver or Flash. Available at http://www.macromedia.com/software/fireworks.

KidPix. Children can use this software program to create images. Includes drawing, coloring, and stamping tools. Available at http://www.kidpix.com.

Paint Shop Pro. This software from JASC provides many of the same features as Photoshop but at a lower cost. Available at http://www.jasc.com.

INTERACTIVE CONTENT CREATION

Adobe Live Motion. This is Adobe's entry into the interactive software field. Available at http://www.adobe.com/products/livemotion/main.html.

Flash. Create high-tech interactive images, movies, animations, and so on with Macromedia Flash. Available at http://www.macromedia.com/software/flash.

Hot Potatoes. Use this tool to create multiple-choice content. Available from Half Baked Software at http://web.uvic.ca/hrd/halfbaked.

Viewlet Builder. Use this tool to animate computer screen/keyboard sequences. Available from Qarbon at http://www.qarbon.com.

WEB-BUILDING SOFTWARE

Adobe GoLive. This is Adobe's entry into the web-building software world. Available at http://www.adobe.com/products/golive/main.html.

Arachnophilia. This free software can be downloaded to a computer and used to write HTML code. Available at http://www.arachnoid.com/arachnophilia.

BBEdit. This software is for MAC users to use when writing HTML code. Available from Bare Bones Software at http://www.barebones.com/index.shtml.

Dreamweaver. Macromedia's state-of-the-art web development software package is at http://www.macromedia.com/software/dreamweaver.

Homesite. Also by Macromedia, Homesite is a less-expensive and easy-to-use tool for creating web pages. Available at http://www.macromedia.com/software/homesite.

Technology Youth Participation Projects in and out of the Library

Below is a list of organizations that are integrating technology into their youth participation projects. It is not a comprehensive list and does not include projects discussed in the body of *Technically Involved*.

Chicago Public Library Tech 37. At the Chicago Public Library high school juniors and seniors receive technology training that they then use to teach patrons how to use computers successfully. The teens also create webliographies on a variety of topics. Learn more about Tech 37 at http://www.chipublib.org/008subject/003cya/teened/tech37intro.html.

Computer Clubhouse. Computer Clubhouses are in underserved communities and work towards giving children and teens the technology skills they need in order to be successful in adulthood. One of the organization's projects, Beyond Four Walls, helps teens use technology as a means of developing competence in science. Information on Computer Clubhouse is available at http://www.computer-clubhouse.org/index.htm. Information on Beyond Four Walls is available at http://www.computerclubhouse.org/programs/ b4w/b4whome.html.

Magis Institute. The Magis Institute is a joint project of Cheverus High School in Portland, Maine, and the Phoenix Foundation. Students who attend the project in the summer learn HTML skills and apply their new skills to developing a website for a community agency, organization, or business. Their portfolio includes Children's Theatre of Maine and the Portland Humanities Committee. The project website is at http://www.magisinstitute.org/ default.asp.

Plugged In Enterprises. This subsidiary of Plugged In, a creative arts and technology project for kids, trains children and teens web design skills and then provides opportunities for use of those skills in developing websites for paying clients. The client list includes Pacific Bell and East Palo Alto Law Project. The Plugged In Enterprises website says this about the work of the kids involved in the project:

> The employment experience is one of working in a real business environment. The teens operate a web page production business and develop web sites for paying clients earning money for their work. They

are evaluated by their supervisors, critiqued by their clients, and "incentivized" to keep abreast of new developments in the field. Their hourly pay is dependent on skill level and ability to transfer skills to peers on the production team, as well as to other teens in the community.

More information on Plugged In Enterprises is available at http://www.pluggedin. org/pie/index.html.

Teen CyberCenter, Haverhill Public Library, Haverhill, Mass. Teen volunteers assist patrons with computers, take computer reservations, and help out with the maintenance of the CyberCenter website. More information on the CyberCenter is available at http://www.teencybercenter.org/tcc/tccinfo.htm. The form for volunteering is also available online at http://www.teencybercenter.org/tcc/vol.htm.

BIBLIOGRAPHY

The materials listed here include items that were discussed or noted in each chapter, along with other resources of interest to those working on youth participation or technology-based youth participation projects for the library.

104th Cong., S.673. *Youth Development Community Block Grant Act of 1995.* Available at http://thomas.loc.gov/cgi-bin/query/F?c104:1:./temp/ ~c104SwyDbq:e1591.

Angelis, Jane. *Intergenerational Service Learning.* Carbondale: Southern Illinois University, 1990.

At the Table: Youth Voices in Decision Making [home page]. Available at http://www.atthetable.org/default.asp.

Camino, Linda A. "Youth-Adult Partnerships: Entering New Territory in Community Work and Research." *Applied Developmental Science* (2000 Supplement): 11–21.

Caywood, Caroline A., ed. *Youth Participation in School and Public Libraries: It Works.* Chicago: ALA, 1995.

Center for Youth Development and Policy Research. "What Is Youth Development?" Available at http://cyd.aed.org/whatis.html.

Central Rappahannock Regional Library. "Web Surfers." Available at http://www. teenspoint.org/free_programs/web_surfers/index.asp.

Chelton, Mary K. *Excellence in Library Services to Young Adults: The Nation's Top Programs.* Chicago: ALA, 1994.

———. *Excellence in Library Services to Young Adults: The Nation's Top Programs.* 2d ed. Chicago: ALA, 1997.

———. *Excellence in Library Services to Young Adults: The Nation's Top Programs.* 3d ed. Chicago: ALA, 2000.

Foundation for Young Australians. "Youth Partnership and Participation." Available at http://www.youngaustralians.org/Resources/Youth%20Participation/ Youth%20Participation.htm.

Freechild Project. "Survey of International Youth Involvement." 2003. Available at http://www.freechild.org/SIYI.

Golombek, Silvia, ed. *What Works in Youth Participation: Case Studies from Around the World.* Baltimore: International Youth Foundation, 2001. Available at http://www.iyfnet.org/pdf/what_works_in_youth_par.pdf.

Hart, Roger. *Children's Participation: From Tokenism to Citizenship.* Innocenti Essay no. 4. Florence: Unicef International Child Development Center, 1992.

Himmel, Ethel, and William James Wilson. *Planning for Results: A Public Library's Transformation Proccess.* Chicago: Public Library Association, 1998.

Innovation Center for Community and Youth Development [home page]. Available at http://www.theinnovationcenter.org.

Jones, Patrick. *Connecting Young Adults and Libraries.* 2d ed. New York: Neal-Schuman, 1998.

Leifer, Loring, and Michael McLarney. "Making the Case for Youth Participation." 1997. Available at http://www.energizeinc.com/art/ayou.html.

Lippmann, Ellen, and Steve Arbuss. *Youth Participation in School and Public Libraries.* Boston: National Commission on Resources for Youth, Inc., 1983.

Maryland Governor's Office on Service and Volunteerism. "Best Practices for Developing a Volunteer Program." Available at http://www.gosv.state. md.us/pubs/bestprac/sec00.htm.

Moore, David W., Thomas W. Bean, Deanna Birdyshaw, and James A. Rycik. *Adolescent Literacy: A Position Statement for the Commission on Adolescent Literacy.* Washington, D.C.: International Reading Association, 1999. Available at http://www.reading.org/pdf/1036.pdf. Summary available at http://www.ira. org/positions/adol_lit.html.

National Academy for Teaching and Learning about Aging. "Planning Intergenerational Programs." Available at http://www.cps.unt.edu/natla/ web/planning_intergenerational_progr.htm.

National Public Radio. *Morning Edition.* "Foster Trip to Ghana," February 13, 2003. Available at http://discover.npr.org/rundowns/rundown.jhtml?prgId= 3&prgDate=February/13/2003.

National Youth Development Information Center. "Definitions of Youth Development." 2000. Available at http://www.nydic.org/nydic/devdef.html.

New York Public Library. "Computer Page Profiles: Success Stories." Available at http://www.nypl.org/branch/ref/pages/profiles.htm.

Public Health Sciences/Centre for Health Promotion. "How Does Meaningful Youth Participation Work to Improve the Health of Youth?" 2001. Available at http://www.canadian-health-network.ca/html/newnotable/apr1_2001e.html.

Public Libraries as Partners in Youth Development [home page of the Urban Libraries Council]. Available at http://www.urbanlibraries.org/plpydhome.html.

Rhodes, Naomi J., and Judith M. Davis. "Using Service Learning to Get Positive Reactions in the Library." *Computers in Libraries* 21 (January 2001): 32–35.

Search Institute. "Forty Developmental Assets for Adolescents." Available at http://www.search-institute.org/assets/forty.htm.

Servenet.org [home page]. Available at http://www.servenet.org.

Terry, Alice W. "An Early Glimpse: Service Learning from an Adolescent Perspective." *Journal of Secondary Gifted Education.* 11 (Spring 2000): 115–126.

Tucillo, Diane. *VOYA Guide to Teen Advisory Boards.* Scarecrow Press, 2003.

"Two Generations of Partners in Prevention." *Youth in Action Bulletin* 5 (July 1999): 2–9.

Vaillancourt, Renee J. *Bare Bones Young Adult Library Services: Tips for Public Library Generalists.* Chicago: ALA, 2000.

———. *Managing Young Adult Services: A Self-Help Manual.* New York: Neal-Schuman, 2002.

Wolf, Maura, and Robert Lewis Jr. "Cultivating Greatness." *Community Youth Development Journal* 2, no. 2 (spring 2001). Available at http://cydjournal. org/2001Spring/wolf.html.

Young Adult Library Services Association with Patrick Jones. *New Directions for Library Service to Young Adults.* Chicago: ALA, 2002.

Young, Karen S., and Jenny Sazama. *Fourteen Points: Successfully Involving Youth in Decision Making.* Somerville, Mass.: Youth on Board, 1999.

Youth Service America [home page]. Available at http://www.ysa.org.

INDEX